FerrariDesign
THE DEFINITIVE STUDY

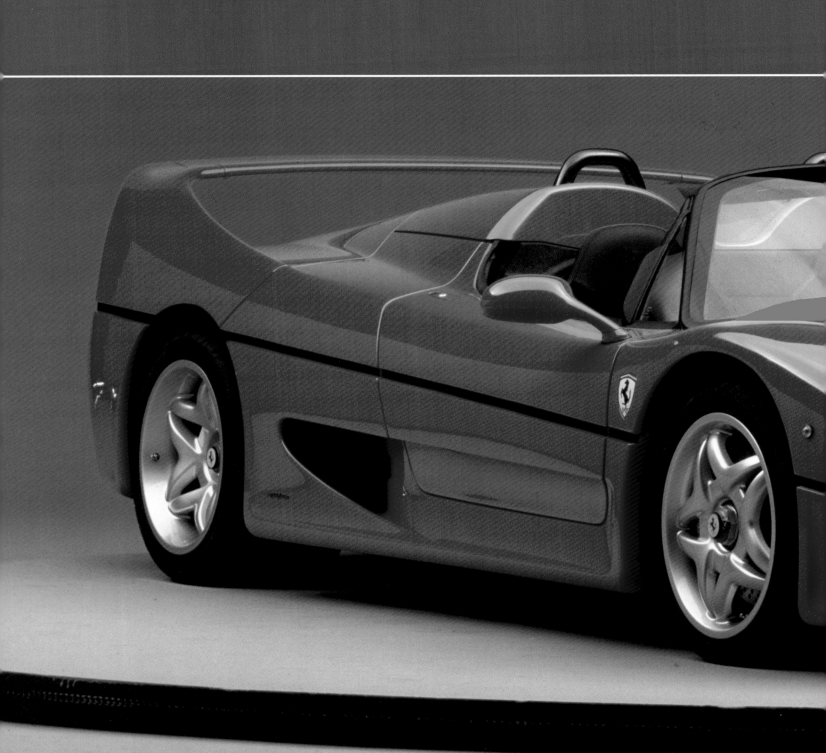

FerrariDesign
THE DEFINITIVE STUDY

Glen Smale

Published in October 2010

A catalogue record for this book is available from the British Library

ISBN 978 1 84425 487 3

Library of Congress control no. 210924934

Published by Haynes Publishing, Sparkford, Yeovil, Somerset BA22 7JJ, UK
Tel: 01963 442030 Fax: 01963 440001
Int. tel: +44 1963 442030
Int. fax: +44 1963 440001
E-mail: sales@haynes.co.uk
Website: www.haynes.co.uk

Haynes North America, Inc.,
861 Lawrence Drive,
Newbury Park,
California 91320, USA

Design and layout by Rod Teasdale

Printed and bound in the USA

Contents

Foreword by Nick Mason

I think it's true to say that Ferrari has made plenty of bad cars, but also many great ones. At the same time, it's arguable that Ferrari almost never made any ugly ones.

Even the cars that left some great drivers shaking with fear, and ones that left fuming customers stranded at the side of the road, were often so breathtakingly beautiful that all could be, and was, forgiven. I shall avoid any cheap jokes about comparisons to women at this point...

For many years Ferrari could not be credited with being a leader in terms of technical development. Their engines were frequently superb, but chassis design and the implementation of any new technology such as disc brakes or mid-engine layouts were often well behind the competition. In some ways the coachwork arrangements were even more retro, in that it was not done in-house but contracted out, in a manner more reminiscent of the vintage era, to the design houses of Italy.

Initially Touring designed the bodies, but was soon joined by Ghia, Vignale and Scaglietti, although once Pinin Farina got his foot in the door the others tended to fall by the wayside, despite Mr Ferrari's penchant for allowing the designers to compete against each other.

And yet these engines, along with the work of the designers, created a brand that is the envy of every single other car manufacturer in the world. Not only that but these designs have, in many cases, become so iconic that they transcend obsolescence. Most auto enthusiasts take as much pleasure in the shape of a Lusso, Daytona or GTO as in the very latest supercars.

Ferrari has even managed to end up owning a colour to signify all that the marque stands for. Ferrari Red is as well known as Navy Blue at a global level.

Good, or great, design is being able not only to clothe the chassis in an aerodynamically efficient shape but to sculpt in some indefinable element that expresses the function of the vehicle.

Even now in the 21st century, where the computer and wind tunnel have become the dictators of shape and form, Ferrari and its designers continue to triumph.

This book looks at the well-trodden Ferrari story from an altogether different angle, by analysing the inspiration (both cultural and technical) and the evolution of Ferrari design over the last sixty-odd years. It also encompasses the changes that became necessary with technical revolutions in material and aerodynamic flow dynamics, which have played an increasingly vital role in car design over the last thirty years. And perhaps most interesting of all, this book considers the future direction of Ferrari design in the 21st century.

Nick Mason

◑ **Nick Mason negotiates the esses at Goodwood in his 250 GTO.** *(LAT)*

Acknowledgements

In researching and writing this book I sought the help of professional designers and commentators, and I would like to make special mention of, and express my gratitude to:

Keith Helfet, who was responsible for the Jaguar XJ220, as well as the F-type and XK180 concepts.

Emanuele Nicosia, design director of BEESTUDIO in Italy, who fielded countless requests to explain certain design concepts and who supplied several previously unpublished images from his own collection.

Professor Dale Harrow, Head of Vehicle Design, Royal College of Art, London, who spent many hours being interviewed and responding to questions on vehicle design.

Collectively I spent many enjoyable hours in the company of these generous and very knowledgeable professionals.

I thank those very helpful and well-informed motoring journalists and photographers who not only supplied material, but were grilled on their contributions to the point of frustration. These long-suffering folk include Anne Hope (Motor Industry Archives), Neill Bruce (Ferrari photographer for many years), Marián Šuman-Hreblay, Doug Nye (automotive historian), Douglas Jamieson (Coys), and Ferrari Owners Club members, Peter Everingham and Jonathan Tremlett.

My thanks also go to photographers James Mann, John Colley, Tom Wood, and Simon Clay, and to Tim Wright from LAT Photographic.

Hannes Oosthuizen of *CAR* magazine in South Africa sourced some valuable images for me from their archives, for which I thank him, and I am also grateful to the staff at the Ford archives in Detroit for providing relevant images.

From the wider automobile industry, I must mention Jason Harris, Head of Communications Ferrari UK; Silvia Pini, Head of Communications Maserati UK; Puneet Joshi, Press Officer Fiat UK; Juliet Jarvis, PR and Press Officer Marketing Lamborghini UK; and Wouter Melissen of Ultimatecarpage. In addition, I would like to thank Silvana Appendino and Simona Penna, of Pininfarina in Turin, for their help in supplying information relating to that company.

Mike Osgood, a bank of knowledge on all matters relating to Ferrari sports cars, spent many hours identifying different models and providing answers to my numerous requests for 'more info'. And David and James Cottingham of DK Engineering, the folk at RM Auctions, and David Gooding, auctioneers in the USA, also provided help, and for this I thank them.

I would also like to thank Nick Mason, who wrote the foreword to this book, and spent hours on the phone answering questions about owning and driving Ferraris. His experience and knowledge in this field was a great help.

Derek Smith and Christine Smith at Haynes were a great support and encouragement, and I would like to thank Editorial Director Mark Hughes, who shared my fascination for the topic of this book.

Last, and by no means least, I would like to mention my family who have once again played their part both directly and indirectly. A huge thank you to Margaux (who helped with interview transcriptions) and Robert (who helped with photo selection) – both are media students, so their knowledge was of greater value than perhaps they realised. And an equally huge thank you to my wife, Elke (who transcribed many hours of interview tapes and supplied countless cups of coffee at all times of the day and night): your contribution was immense.

Ferrari F430 Spider photographed at the Spa Francorchamps circuit, August 2008. *(Author)*

Introduction

Maranello, a small town by most standards, sits in the northern Italian province of Modena. With a population of little more than 15,000, it must boast the happiest sub-group of people on the planet, that of the many young schoolboys who long to one day work for their beloved Ferrari 'stabilimento'. Demonstrating a passion that borders on total devotion, 'bambinos' walking to and from school press their faces to the fencing as they watch their favourite red cars being wheeled around the plant or tested on the famous Fiorano track.

What is it about Ferrari cars that they are considered by so many enthusiasts to be special and a cut above the rest in the sports car industry? Is it because they built up such a dominant reputation from winning so many races over the years that their road cars became equally fearsome in the minds of car lovers? Or is it, perhaps, that no one in the industry could fully get the measure of Enzo Ferrari, the man. It is surely this, and more.

Certainly, there was no mistaking the fanatical respect that the locals had for these cars and, as Ferrari's reputation grew, this passion spread to millions around the world. Passion, though, is not something that can be pulled off the shelf and bolted on to a car, rather it has to be earned by the perseverance and commitment of all involved in the design and manufacturing process.

Lightweight construction, powerful engines and sleek, streamlined bodywork all became the hallmarks of the Ferrari sports car legend, and with an unrivalled design and styling industry on its doorstep, it is not surprising that over the years Ferrari have produced some of the most desirable sports cars in the world. Indeed, if a car can be described as having a personality, it is the Ferrari.

The finest Italian automotive design studios vied with each other for the opportunity to put their stamp on the cars from Maranello, but one name dominates this aspect of the Ferrari story. That name is Carrozzeria Pinin Farina (later Pininfarina), and their creativity in establishing a successful design language for Ferrari's cars played a crucial role in the growth of the Ferrari brand – and in the process Pininfarina gained for themselves worldwide renown.

Enzo Ferrari was never one to readily change his ways – he was the last manufacturer to move from a front-engined Formula 1 layout to the mid-engined style in 1961 – so, not surprisingly, he was reluctant to experiment with the mid-engined Dino concept in 1967. This development would only become part of the Ferrari legend through the introduction of the revolutionary 308 GTB, a model that sent the Italian manufacturer on an altogether new course in sports car design.

Although the mid-engined sports car genre reshaped the Maranello manufacturer, Ferrari never lost its desire to produce front-engined grand tourers, and in the 1990s the company returned to its roots with the introduction of the 456 GT. Advances in technology opened the doors for a string of grand tourers following the trendsetting 456, and Ferrari was able to add a new range to the mid-engined cars that had dominated for some years. Throughout this time it is hard to single out any poor models, but there have been those Ferraris that have not been admired by the public quite as much as had been hoped by the factory, yet they still played their part in the stylistic evolution of the brand.

Including interviews with Pininfarina designers, and many unseen images, this revealing study, covering 60-plus years, provides an interesting and thought-provoking insight into a much overlooked aspect of Ferrari's history – the design evolution of one of the world's most admired sports cars. Happy reading.

⟲ **The Enzo Ferrari is a technical and aerodynamic powerhouse.** *(Author)*

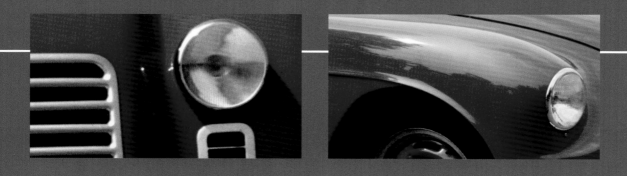

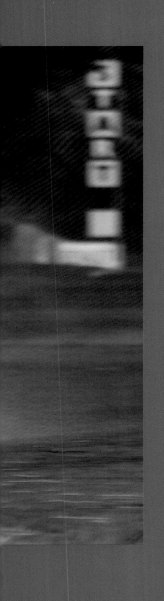

'Nuovo inizio'
– NEW BEGINNINGS

They were virtually handmade suits of armour, really, but just made into cars. Fantastic!

– PROFESSOR DALE HARROW
Head of Vehicle Design, Royal College of Art, London

How it all began

Why Italy? Why is it that so many of the world's most admired and beautifully designed and engineered motor cars come from Italy? Professor Dale Harrow, Head of Vehicle Design at the Royal College of Art, London, offers this explanation: 'I think what actually drove the Italian revolution was the way they were designing things at the time. If you look at Turin itself and the surrounding area, it was basically a place of metalwork. They made suits of armour in this region during the 14th and 15th centuries, so there were a lot of very good metalwork skills in that area, and I think the way they were designing cars [in the period 1940–60] is very much associated with this craft process.'

Also, Italy had long been recognised internationally as a centre for excellence in art and sculpture. Ross Ashmore, art and design critic (and classic sports car enthusiast) explains: 'In the 18th and 19th centuries, British gentry toured Italy to visit art galleries and museums to further their education – a travel rite that became known as the Grand Tour. Italian art was an important inspiration and influence during the Regency period.'

⋂ **Baconino Borzacchini, Enzo Ferrari, and Tazio Nuvolari standing alongside a racing Alfa (1920s).** *(LAT)*

More recently, the country's recovery following the Second World War saw Italian manufacturers' striving for aesthetic and technical innovation. Their efforts were duly rewarded by rapid growth in demand for the stylish modern products from a range of mould-breaking designers, not least from the automotive industry, and subsequent international recognition put Italy at the leading edge of modern design.

Ferrari in the 1940s

Any kid between the age of 5 and 95 will tell you that Ferrari sports cars are the fastest in the world and definitely the best looking. At least that was the view of devoted Ferrari followers around the world throughout the second half of the last century. It is a reputation built up over many years in which the red Ferrari racing cars were dominant in most race categories, and in most countries where they raced.

Enzo Ferrari, like many other self-styled entrepreneurs in the 20th century who were destined to head up their own motor manufacturing empires, started at the bottom of the ladder and, through hard work and perseverance, effectively wrote his own future. Names such as Porsche, Ford, Bugatti, Austin, Lamborghini, Rolls and Royce, are those of automotive visionaries who were way ahead of their time. Each of them, Ferrari included, possessed foresight and an inner strength beyond mere determination.

Common amongst the industry names mentioned above, and many of their contemporaries in this field, was the ability to surround themselves with knowledgeable and experienced engineers and designers capable of

turning ideas into a winning formula. Another common factor was their fascination with early motor sport, an activity in which many of them participated personally, and it is possibly this that enabled many of those budding entrepreneurs to develop an appreciation for engineering, and an understanding of how they thought they could improve the cars they were manufacturing.

Ferrari began his employment at 22 at the Anonima Lombarda Fabbrica Automobili (ALFA) factory in 1920 as an official works driver for the Alfa team (1923), but in 1929 he set up Scuderia Ferrari S.A., which effectively operated as Alfa's racing department for the next ten years. It provided cars and engineering, technical, and design services when Alfa's own resources were stretched to the limit.

In 1938 things changed when Alfa Romeo returned to running its own racing activities, setting up a dedicated in-house racing division known as Alfa Corse, and absorbing Scuderia Ferrari as a new division in the process. Alfa's relationship with Enzo Ferrari continued and he became a consultant to the new organisation, with responsibility for designing and developing new racing cars – an arrangement, however, which only lasted for a year.

It had long been Ferrari's goal to manufacture his own racing cars, but in 1939 when he made his break he had to accept a four-year ban on using his own name on his cars, as his previous employers were well aware of the considerable reputation he had built up in the motor-racing world.

Ferrari's first car, the Vettura 815 (two roadsters were made), was constructed under the name of Ferrari's machine tool company, Auto Avio Costruzioni, in Modena in 1940. Fiat components formed the basis of the 815, and the chassis and 1496cc in-line eight-cylinder engine were derived from the Fiat 508 C Balilla 1100. The smooth lines of the 815 were the work of Carrozzeria Touring, of Milan, a style which owed much to the Alfa Romeo 6C 2500 of 1939, but which also showed some similarities with the BMW 328 of 1936.

For most coachbuilders at that time, work would begin on a bare chassis received from a manufacturer. Using small-diameter metal tubing, the carrozzeria's craftsmen would first construct a frame closely resembling the shape of the car's body. This would then be welded to the chassis, and the aluminium body panels were formed over this frame by hand,

⌒ Ferrari's first sports car, the Auto Avio Costruzioni 815 of 1940. *(LAT)*

or by mechanical hammers, and finally welded to the supporting tubular frame. The resulting structure was a rigid but lightweight body.

Carrozzeria Touring, Italy's most prestigious designer and manufacturer of car bodies at the time, was known to Ferrari from his Alfa Romeo days, when the coachbuilder was responsible for building an incredible variety of street and race-winning competition cars.

In many ways, the work done by Touring complemented Ferrari's own style, as their designs were not only attractive, but also extremely weight efficient. Touring refined the familiar fabrication method described above, and the Milanese designer became well known for its 'Superleggera' (Italian for 'very light')

coachbuilding. Touring's patented fabrication method consisted of an inner framework of steel tubes, while the outer panels would be formed over a wooden buck (a full-scale model of the car made of wood). The panels were then fastened to the framework by rolling the panel edges around the tubing, thereby forming an extremely strong and lightweight structure – ideal for racing.

With the onset of war, Ferrari was forced to put on hold his dream of becoming a racing car manufacturer in his own right, but when peacetime returned he wasted no time in picking up where he had left off in 1940. The first car to bear his name, the 1.5-litre V12 125 S, debuted in 1947.

⋒ **The first car to bear Ferrari's name, the 1.5-litre V12 125 S, which debuted in 1947.** *(LAT)*

In Ferrari's world the 1940s were characterised by a few very talented and carefully handpicked individual racing drivers, as this period would see the emergence of the fully-fledged professional racing driver who required top-rate machinery with which to win races. Professional racing drivers did nothing else but race and they could not simply return to alternative sources of employment in a 'nine-to-five' job following a bad race. In the sport of motor racing, if you made it as a driver you were hailed as a national hero, but if you failed there were few who would offer gainful employment to a wannabe racing driver. This left out in the cold the rich but talented amateur drivers of the '20s and '30s for whom racing had been a glorified hobby or an extension of their social lives, as the sport had moved on considerably since then.

Higher performing sports cars competing in the international arena could only be developed through the constant attentions of a professionally equipped race department and with the financial resources of a large manufacturer. And, since manufacturers' race teams were sufficiently well prepared and equipped to enter and participate in an increasing number of races across Europe, there was a need for the full-time commitment of professional racing drivers.

In time, manufacturers began to rely on the increasingly professional services of top-rate international drivers with whom they could be seen to win races, and at the same time test the reliability of their products. These manufacturers also began to see the commercial value of winning and having their name in the press and other news media of those early days, such as the Pathé News, which ran in cinemas before a main feature film. This offered manufacturers an ideal opportunity to capture the attention of an emotionally charged younger generation, for whom the cinema was an important attraction and gathering place. As a result, racing drivers were increasingly relied upon to carry the name of the manufacturer into the spotlight through winning, and this normally involved national pride at the highest level.

Following the end of the Second World War Italy had to rebuild its economic power base, and the late 1940s was a period of renaissance based on the engineering lessons learned during the war – it was found that many aeronautical innovations could be used to good effect in motor racing applications. For instance, the use of aluminium and the riveting of body panels (as with

Origins of the 'Prancing Horse' emblem

The famous symbol of the Ferrari stable is a black prancing horse on a yellow background, enclosed within a shield. This is usually accompanied by the letters S F, which stand for Scuderia Ferrari.

The prancing (or more accurately 'rearing up') horse was originally the symbol of Count Francesco Baracca, a legendary Italian air ace during the First World War. Baracca painted this emblem on the fuselage of his fighter plane because his squad, the Battaglione Aviatori, formed part of the Cavalry regiment, as the Italian air force was in its infancy and did not then have its own command.

Besides being a skilled rider himself, it was known that Baracca came from a noble family which owned many horses. Interestingly, the Porsche emblem would later also include a rampant horse, as that manufacturer was located in Stuttgart, a city built over the early remains of a stud farm, hence the name Stutengarten (or Gestüt) and eventually Stuttgart. The term 'stud farm' translates from the original German into 'scuderia' in Italian from where we get the 'Ferrari stable' today.

Baracca died in 1918 when he was shot down, but his rampant horse emblem lives on in another scuderia, the House of Ferrari.

↶ A 'Prancing Horse' badge showing 'S F' initials. *(Author)*

the Jaguar C-type and D-type), and other lightweight construction methods, was technology transferred from wartime aircraft manufacture.

A profound shift in the course of post-war European car design was signalled by the demise of coachbuilding in almost every country except Italy. There were a number of reasons for this, including the devastation of premises during the years of conflict, the migration of skills, and a seismic shift downwards in the demand for expensive automobiles. Most of all though it was the swing away from the traditional separate chassis and body towards unitary body construction. But art and creative skills have always flourished in Italy and that nation was not about to lose this traditional craft handed down through the generations. So, in the Italian automotive industry, coachbuilding survived through the evolution of a new approach to vehicle design, one that incorporated both low volume specials and conventional production cars.

From racing to road cars

In 1943 the Ferrari factory moved from its original site in Modena to Maranello (18km/11 miles to the north), where it has remained ever since. The plant, which was bombed in 1944, was rebuilt in 1946 to include a separate works for road car production, but right up to Enzo Ferrari's death on 14 August 1988, this would remain little more than a source of funding for his first love, racing.

Ferrari's philosophy was always to combine the efficiency of a streamlined, lightweight body with a powerful engine, thereby creating a high-performance sporting package. Attracted by the performance possibilities of 12-cylinders, Ferrari sought to explore the potential of this engine format in his own cars, as he had already seen what the four, six and eight-cylinder engines were capable of in the Alfa cars. And it was the V12 engine that was to become the hallmark of Ferrari cars for many years, an engine which had powered the first car to bear Ferrari's name, the 125 S.

Right from the very first cars that Ferrari manufactured, the little 815 and the 125 S, the factory has used some measure of the engine specification in the model naming. For instance, the 815 referred to its 8 cylinders and its 1.5-litre capacity, while the 125 designation represented the swept volume in cubic centimetres of one cylinder of the all-aluminium V12, giving a total engine capacity of 1500cc. This legendary engine was designed by

Gioachino Colombo, an ex-Alfa colleague from Ferrari's days with that company.

The 125 S and the model that followed, the bigger-engined 159 S, were both cars built with competition in mind. The 159 model (which proved that a 1.9-litre V12 was a reliable engine) was, however, an interim model built between the 125 and the 166 that came out in 1948. By the time that the 159 had arrived on the scene, its styling had already moved away from the enclosed cycle-wing style, and now incorporated a smoother, more rounded and purposeful racing design.

Ferrari cars were for the privileged minority, and very few, if any, road cars were produced. It was more a case of modifying the odd Ferrari race car into a road-legal form than planning for a limited production run of such sports cars.

The 166 S was the first Ferrari car not intended exclusively for competition, and three of these were built over the winter of 1947/8. The new styling of the first two cars, by Allemano, was a combination of both road and race car, and was described as 'ungainly' because of its wider and flatter shape with a rather unimaginative square-shaped grille, which did little to enhance the car's broad looks. Despite its apparent heaviness, a 166 S Allemano was driven to victory in the 1948 Targa Florio, while a coupé version (Ferrari's first enclosed body) won the Mille Miglia that year. The third car was designed by Touring of Milan and would prove a good indicator for the forthcoming 166 Inter, only due for release a year later.

Despite racking up the victories, Ferrari's cars were just like all the other manufacturers' cars of the day – high on performance but rather bland and faceless. Both Ferrari and Touring recognised that their new cars needed to give Ferrari a distinctive face, something that would make the Modenese cars stand out from the rest of the pack and earn the company the respect that Ferrari desired. It wouldn't be until the arrival of the Touring-designed 166 MM Barchetta (little boat) that Ferrari would achieve this recognisable identity.

It was the work of none other than Carlo Felice Bianchi Anderloni (1916–2003) who, it is said, grew up with automotive design in his blood. Anderloni had seen first-hand how the business of car designing was done, as his father was design director at Carrozzeria Touring, and when Anderloni senior died suddenly in 1948, it fell to his son to create the car that would establish the

face of Ferrari. With hindsight, this was an awesome responsibility as all Ferraris ultimately developed in one way or another from this seed.

The 166 series was to become the foundation on which Ferrari built his reputation as a sports and race car manufacturer. Regarded by the media as a style that was refreshingly new, Ferrari's 166 MM Touring Barchetta was unveiled at the Turin Motor Show on 15 September 1948, and featured a body-length rib at waist height that added both strength and style to the open two-seater. The 166 MM that followed was to win the prestigious 24-hour races at Le Mans and Spa, and the Mille Miglia, all in 1949. The 166 MM, by Touring of Milan, a compact and very capable racer, was already showing signs of attractive styling, although one example by Zagato had such large windows that it resembled a greenhouse.

⋒ **Ferrari's 166 formed the foundation of several highly-successful models between 1948 and 1949. Joining the front and rear wheel-arches was a strengthening rib that gave the otherwise plain flanks some shape. This is the 166 MM by Touring (1948) seen at the Goodwood Festival of Speed in 2006.** *(Author)*

⟃ **This 1949 Ferrari 166 Inter by Touring already shows signs of a flowing style, although it still features a split windscreen.** *(Geoffrey Goddard © Neill Bruce)*

⌒ 1950 Ferrari 166 MM/195 S Berlinetta by Touring. Created by Ferrari to compete in the 1950 Le Mans 24-Hour, the 195 S was fitted with a larger 2341cc V12 engine, but the rest of the car was all 166 MM. The body by Touring featured the designer's patented Superleggera lightweight construction method, and with its streamlined body this particular vehicle led the 1950 24-Hour race at Le Mans for 11 hours, before retiring with a broken generator bracket. (Simon Clay)

⌒ From the rear three-quarter angle, the 1949 Ferrari 166 Inter by Touring demonstrates a 'fastback' design that was well ahead of most of the market. (Geoffrey Goddard © Neill Bruce)

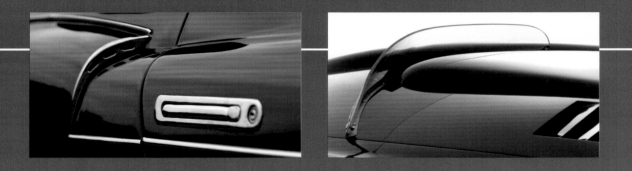

The legend begins

At a certain point it became clear that one of us was looking for a lovely and renowned woman to dress, and the other was looking for a world-class couturier to clothe her, Enzo Ferrari reminisced.

— ANTOINE PRUNET
Pininfarina Art and Industry 1930–2000

Ferrari in the 1950s

A new decade dawned with a fresh impetus. Ferrari beefed up the 166 by increasing the engine size by 17%, from 1995cc to 2341cc, in the process pushing up power from 140bhp to 170bhp. The new car was called the 195 S and, although the similarities with the 166 were clear, the sports saloon was a particularly handsome vehicle. Styling at Ferrari was certainly an aspect of car manufacture that had come to stay, whether it was a road or a race car.

Nick Mason on the Italian design explosion

What was it that ignited the design revolution, especially in Italy in the '50s and '60s?

'I think it is more to do with social history. Post-war, the Italian design studios went straight into that activity, whereas I don't think British manufacturers ever had that sort of design style and ethic anyway. I think they were more interested in engineering.

'I mean, you can look at very early Italian cars of the '50s which had beautiful lines, whereas the English were still doing Fraser-Nash Le Mans reps. So is there something in the Italian character that makes them a little more flowing in line – is it to do with the olive oil? It is almost certainly in the diet and the weather,' he laughed.

'But,' Mason concluded, 'Ferrari are fairly unique in that virtually every other manufacturer has their own design studio. I would have thought that this has something to do with the independence of the design studios, whether Bertone or Pininfarina, or whatever.'

➲ **In the company's early days, Ferrari was not averse to using several different design houses. This served to keep the element of creativity high as competition in this sector was still keen. This 1950 two-door 195 Inter Berlinetta is by Ghia (chassis 0060).** *(Neill Bruce)*

If anything, the racing 195 S driven by Marzotto/Crosara and styled by Touring, looked more elegant than the equivalent road-going 195 Inter by Vignale. What this says is that Ferrari's race cars were becoming recognisable for their styling and elegance in spite of the fact that they were intended for the rough and tumble of international motor sport, and were quite likely to get damaged in the course of a race.

At this point in the Ferrari manufacturing story, the company was still primarily concerned with the fabrication of lightweight racing cars. These were traditional front-engined sports racers – this was the only drivetrain layout being used at the time since nobody (except Porsche) had really experimented with any other set-up. If Ferrari looked to any other manufacturers for confirmation that what he was doing was right, he would have seen that Jaguar, Mercedes-Benz, Aston Martin, Allard, Cunningham, and many others, were all developing front-engined, rear-wheel-drive sports cars.

Touring produced the 166 Inter, and Bertone the 166 Inter Cabriolet, and both were shown at the Turin Motor Show in 1950, while Ghia built its first Ferrari body, a classically elegant two-door Berlinetta 195 Inter in the same year.

At the start of the 1950s, the automotive world was on the verge of a design revolution born of creative liberation and a blossoming of ideas, and it led to a wide variety of body styles, even from a single design house, as designers sought to convey the impression of speed, power, and grace through their interpretation of that specific design brief.

Professor Penny Sparke, Dean of the Faculty of Design at Kingston University, London, described it this way: 'Stylistically they learned quickly from pre-war advances made both in the United States and in Europe, combining them to create a stunning new aesthetic hybrid which, characterised by its long, low, racy, sleek, sculptural forms, came to be known as "Italian style".'

However, Ferrari was slow to change, believing that if a race-car set-up worked it should be improved and not changed, and he stayed with front-engined cars longer than most in the industry. At the time, though, with the exception of Porsche, no other major motor manufacturer or race stable considered placing their engine anywhere in the car other than up front.

Penny Sparke again: 'The "supercars" of this era were a result of these companies' ability to straddle the boundary between racing cars and road cars and to bring the thrill and excitement of the former to the latter.'

Such design progression came from the transition of the traditional pre-war coachbuilders' role into a more versatile designer/consulting one, enabling the more adventurous designers to experiment with modern styles and customers' needs. This new-found freedom of expression also gave the manufacturers the opportunity to select those designers who proved to be the best in the industry at adapting to modern trends. Thus was born the modern vehicle design industry.

⊃ The Ferrari 195 Inter Berlinetta by Ghia showed great balance and elegance. *(Neill Bruce)*

⋃ This rear three-quarter view of a two-door Ferrari 195 Inter Berlinetta by Ghia (1950) shows the strong family lineage of the 166 model. *(Neill Bruce)*

The year 1950 seemed to be a point at which one could see a clear sporting identity begin to emerge in Ferrari's cars, as the 195 began to show a purposeful sports styling. With the benefit of hindsight, the styling of the 195 S of 1950 can be seen in the 340 America, 212 Export, 250 S and many other sports and racing models right into the 1960s. Ferrari was able to do this by fitting the same engines in as many models as possible, and the long bonnet style, with the cockpit set well back in the frame, enabled him to achieve this.

If two coachbuilders are to be singled out as making the greatest contribution to Ferrari's long-term styling at this early stage, they would certainly be Touring and Vignale. By 1954, Vignale had built almost 100 bodies, with no two being the same. This type of limited production run suited the exclusive and often very individualistic requirements of many Ferrari drivers.

Vignale's styling for the Modenese cars usually incorporated a long curving body line that extended

below window level from the front wing (fender) right the way through the doors to the rear wings and to the back of the car. Vignale's designer, Giovanni Michelotti, was highly regarded for his ability to create masterful drawings on paper, but it was Vignale himself who translated these drawings directly into metal, without the use of wooden bucks. Body detailing was carefully thought out, even for a sports car with the performance potential of the 195, and individual items such as vents, handles, clasps, and latches were exquisitely crafted into the overall design of the car. Vignale himself made many of these, and he paid extremely high attention to detail and to the quality of overall workmanship – something that no doubt pleased Enzo Ferrari immensely.

Between 1950 and 1953, Vignale was commissioned to clothe the cars of Ferrari's works team, which was victorious in three Mille Miglia races (1951: Ferrari 340 America Berlinetta; 1952: Ferrari 250 S Berlinetta; 1953: Ferrari 340 MM). In the 1951 Carrera Panamericana in Mexico, Vignale-bodied Ferrari 212s finished in first and second place, while the following year a Vignale Ferrari 340 Mexico finished in third place behind a pair of works Mercedes. The final running of this legendary race in 1954 saw another Ferrari one-two finish, when the powerful 375 Plus, bodied by Pinin Farina and driven by Umberto Maglioli, took the flag, with a similar Vignale-bodied car, driven by Phil Hill, in second place.

Vignale was still doing a lot of the coachbuilding for the owners of Ferrari sports cars, and in 1951 his attentions shifted from the longer-wheelbase (2,500mm) cars to the shorter-wheelbase (2,250mm) competition models for Ferrari themselves. One such model was the 212 Export of 1951, which was available as the Inter, being for road use, while the Export was predominantly for competition. The creation of the 212 Export, which debuted at the 1951 Geneva Motor Show in cabriolet form, provided evidence that Ferrari was eyeing the US market with a view to increasing its presence there.

⌒ **This 1950 Ferrari 166/195 Inter has a Michelotti-designed body by Vignale. The 195 was a development of the 166 but with the engine enlarged to 2340cc. Originally purchased in April 1950, the car was returned to the Ferrari factory in September the following year and upgraded to 195 specifications.** *(Tom Wood)*

It should be remembered that this was only six years after the end of the Second World War, and cars manufactured up until that time, by and large, featured designs carried over from pre-war days. Even the fabulous Jaguar XK120 and the BMW328 still carried strong links to the earlier and more pronounced wing (fender) styling, as brand names with a longer tradition in production were more cautious about introducing design innovations, instead seeking to prolong aspects of 'timeless elegance' with which the market was familiar, while 'dabbling' with some new elements. So general body proportions were not dissimilar to those of pre-war models. When the Ferrari 166 and 212 were introduced, however, they represented the epitome of sports car design, as designers of Ferrari cars moved towards the Flow Shell style, as also seen in the Porsche 356, Alfa Romeos, and Lancias of the period.

Ferrari's production line, though, did not extend to more than perhaps a few dozen cars a year at this stage, and as they were all hand made, no two of the same model were the same. This is in stark contrast to production at Maranello today, where the vastly increased production across all models results in identical cars differing perhaps only in the list of options selected by the prospective client.

Flow Shell design

In the early 1950s there was little distinction between the design of road and race cars, and it was not uncommon to compete in motor sport events in a normal family saloon (sedan). It was during this period that European manufacturers began exploring the benefits of improved aerodynamics and how this could enhance the performance of cars in competition.

Early steps in the direction of more sleek designs resulted in the creation of the Grand Touring body style, which, as its name suggests, was intended for touring the roads of Europe in comfort and at speed. The resultant shape enabled the air to 'flow' off the back of the body, thereby creating the Flow Shell design.

General characteristics of this design form incorporated a lower bonnet line that typically

© 1956 Porsche 356A
Carrera Coupé.

(Porsche Werkfoto)

◆ 1951 Ferrari 212
Export Berlinetta Le
Mans by Touring of
Milan – Chassis 0112E.

(Neill Bruce)

sat below the level of the wings (fenders), clean body-lines and good driving visibility thanks to generous-sized windscreens and side glass. The flowing style of the body would taper towards the rear allowing the air to slip off the body with the least resistance. This style was the hallmark of most top European sports car manufacturers throughout the '50s, '60s, and '70s, giving us the 'GT' nomenclature that we associate with sports and many performance-orientated cars today.

Other coachbuilders, such as Fontana of Padua and Rocco Motto of Turin, produced yet more extravagant bodies for Ferrari customers. The Fontana creations included a Barchetta and a Coupé, the latter known as 'The Egg' because of its profoundly round shape, but it was nevertheless an efficient racing design. Fontana's Barchetta, however, received the rather ungracious name of 'Sicilian Cart'.

The 212, built between 1950 and 1953, was a model that enjoyed the attentions of a great many coachbuilders. Among these were Fontana, Motto, Ghia, Ghia Aigle, Pinin Farina, Stabilimenti Farina, Touring, Vignale, and even the British firm Abbott, this last company being responsible for a four-seater cabriolet, which must rank as one of the most ungainly Ferraris ever built. However, Vignale was by far the most prolific Ferrari coachbuilder during the 212's life, being responsible for 37 of the 82 Inters made. Both Vignale and Ghia were making inroads into Touring's share of this market, as the latter company was at this stage making ever fewer Ferrari bodies.

The 1951 212 Export Berlinetta Le Mans by Touring is very similar in design to the 166 of 1949, with the exception of the full-width front windscreen. *(Neill Bruce)*

Touring created a good balance with the 212 Export Berlinetta Le Mans, as the cabin is set well back allowing the engine to sit behind the front axle line. *(Neill Bruce)*

↻ Touring was well known for their Superleggera (superlight) bodywork, as seen on this 1951 212 Export Berlinetta Le Mans. *(Neill Bruce)*

⊃ The 1951 212 Export Berlinetta Le Mans by Touring differed from the 166 in that the bonnet vent had been removed and a pair of air intakes appeared on either side below the headlamps. *(Neill Bruce)*

⊆ This 1951 212 Export Berlinetta by Vignale is set in the grounds of Brocket Hall, one of England's finest stately homes set in rural Hertfordshire. It was home to two British prime ministers and was visited by George IV, so is perhaps a fitting backdrop for this more regal example of Italy's finest. *(Neill Bruce)*

◌ Vignale certainly created a sleek and streamlined body on this 1951 212 Export Berlinetta. *(Neill Bruce)*

◌ The exquisite styling is ably complemented by superb detailing. *(Neill Bruce)*

◌ Not everybody wanted to race their Ferrari – increased comfort and luxury for the export market already showed that Ferrari was aiming his cars at foreign markets. This is the interior of a 1951 Vignale-designed 212 Export Berlinetta. *(Neill Bruce)*

Carrozzeria Vignale

Alfredo Vignale began his career at 17 as assistant panel beater with Stabilimenti Farina where he later became foreman. Managed at that time by Giovanni Farina, the older brother of Pinin Farina, Vignale's first body was the Fiat Topolino.

Vignale established his own 'carrozzeria' (body works) in 1948, and contracts with Lancia, Fiat, and Ferrari followed, eventually making over 100 bodies for the Maranello firm. Vignale and designer Giovanni Michelotti had an extraordinary working partnership in which Vignale could interpret his designer's drawings without the need for scale models. In the mid-1950s Vignale moved into a large modern factory at Grugliasco, near Fiat's Mirafiori works where he also started producing cars under his own name as from 1961, using mainly rolling chassis from Fiat.

He died in a car accident in December 1969, aged just 56, after which his firm was absorbed by Ghia. Carrozzeria Vignale was finally closed in 1974 as a result of the lower than expected sales of the Pantera, by then a product of the Ford empire.

The 340 America designed by Touring, first shown at the Paris Motor Show in October 1951, was seen by Ferrari as a way of creating a sports car for competition but which also showed potential as a grand tourer for his elite clientele, especially across the Atlantic. The sports saloon carried a detuned version of the Lampredi-designed 340 F1 engine, a whopping great 4100cc V12, a fact which was of great public relations value to Ferrari.

The success of the 2.6-litre 212s in the Mexican road race La Carrera Panamericana in 1951 inspired Ferrari to build a more powerful model with which to compete in the sports car class of the 1952 event. The result was the 340 Mexico, a mighty 4.1-litre V12 sports car producing 280bhp, and the intention was to blow away the opposition. The body was designed by Giovanni Michelotti, who was fast becoming the most creative and enterprising automotive designer in Italy, and was once again built by Vignale. For the Mexican race Ferrari had four cars built, three sports saloons, or Berlinettas, and a roadster, but unfortunately engine troubles put two cars out of the running, while one of the Berlinettas came home in third place. The fourth car, the open roadster, did not start.

This quite exotic looking Ferrari 212 De Luxe T.51 by Vignale was initially the property of an Italian nobleman, of whom there were many, all cultivated by Enzo Ferrari to sustain his new boutique manufacturing style. *(John Colley)*

This Ferrari 212 De Luxe T.51 was brought into the UK in the early 1960s by The Chequered Flag dealership in Chiswick, West London, an outfit run by Graham Warner, a very effective racing driver and team patron. Warner sold it to Leicester-based shoebox manufacturer David Clarke. *(John Colley)*

In designing the 340 Mexico, Michelotti pushed the 212's concept even further by positioning the base of the front windscreen just behind the mid-point of the car's wheelbase. The effect of this design was to place the engine in a mid-front position, improving the car's balance and handling, and in the process creating the longest Ferrari bonnet to date, while the low roofline helped the car's overall aerodynamics. In order to manage the airflow around the sides of the car, Michelotti placed a flat wing of metal in a vertical position about 4in behind the front edge of the door, the effect of which was to keep the air that flowed along the car's flanks close to the body, directing it into the air ducts in the rear wings (fenders) for cooling the brakes. Apart from being an efficient design, the 340 was brilliantly stylish, with the strong exit vents in the front wings for expelling hot engine air, finished off with an attractive chrome strip running along the car's waistline to the rear wheel arch.

The front of the car featured the now famous egg-crate grille, the design of which was also credited to Michelotti. The two large headlamps were recessed, while the small indicator lamps were precariously perched on the leading edges of the rather odd, forward

David Clarke, a former Frazer-Nash owner/racer, had become a leading Ferrari enthusiast and connoisseur, and he owned the car for many years. It is perhaps not surprising that this Vignale-styled Ferrari 212 De Luxe T.51 caught his eye, as the front end of the car has a close resemblance to the Frazer-Nash with its in-board headlights. *(John Colley)*

Vignale's attention to detail on this 1951 Ferrari 212 De Luxe T.51 is staggering, and surely lifts this model above others of the same era. *(John Colley)*

protruding wings (fenders). However, Michelotti gave the 340 Mexico an aggressive rear end, a view which was intended mostly for the opposition to see, with two vertical exit vents integrated into the rear wings below the tail lights which allowed hot brake air to escape.

By 1951, Vignale had begun to destabilise Touring's position as the coachbuilder of choice in the world of Ferrari competition cars, while the Turin-based Ghia also continued to build a number of Maranello's street cars. The following year, however, saw Pinin Farina enter the frame, with their first Ferrari-bodied car, a rather stately and conservative 212 Inter convertible. Shown at the Paris Motor Show in late 1952, the Inter convertible was a slightly less sporty grand tourer with style and presence.

That old adage, 'win on Sunday, sell on Monday' could be applied in the case of the Vignale-bodied 212 Inter which won the 1951 Carrera Panamericana in Mexico, bringing considerable media coverage and public interest to the marque. The 212 Inter was a very good seller for Ferrari in America as a result.

Pinin Farina's second model was the rather elegant 342 America, a somewhat lazy detuned version of the 4100cc V12, which offered convertible motoring to a small but select band of American customers.

Although the 225 S enjoyed only a brief lifespan (just one year) this 1952 sports racer carried an important engine – the bigger 2700cc unit. Although it closely resembled its forebear, the 212, the newer car served as an important interim model, as it allowed the factory to concentrate on developing the 3-litre V12 engine.

Automotive technology was moving forward at a fast pace in the 1950s, and the romantic era of coachbuilding was drawing to a close. Two factors signalled the end of this golden era of bespoke bodies for Ferrari cars – cost and an insufficiency of skilled workers – and the 212 Inter was the last model to be bodied by the coachbuilding industry. The following model, the 250 Europa, marked the beginning of a new era which turned out to be very fruitful for both Ferrari and their new-found partners, Pinin Farina.

It was difficult in the beginning to separate the road cars from the competition cars, because Ferrari's sole purpose was to fabricate race cars. If someone wanted a road car, that came lower down the list of priorities and was often just a detuned version of a race car. But the 1950s changed all that, as Ferrari realised that the proceeds from the sale of road cars could significantly help to fund the production of his beloved race cars.

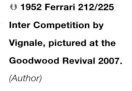

1952 Ferrari 212/225 Inter Competition by Vignale, pictured at the Goodwood Revival 2007.

(Author)

◖ Another fine example of Vignale's work is this stunning 1952 Ferrari 212 Inter Berlinetta. This model, which became known as the 'Bumblebee' because of its distinctive colouring, featured unusual forward-pointing and rather prominent wings (fenders) and as a result, the headlamps were mounted in the grille. *(Simon Clay)*

◠ Vignale built 150 Ferrari bodies between 1950 and 1954. Their attention to detail and finish was without equal at the time, as the very contemporary but attractive and discreet rear fins on this 1952 212 Inter testify. The vent-like aperture on the rear wing (fender) is a light, another example of Vignale's fine handiwork. *(Simon Clay)*

Carrozzeria Pinin Farina

Born in Turin on 2 November 1893, Battista Farina, the youngest of 11 children, worked in his brother Giovanni's body shop, Stabilimenti Farina, from the age of 11. By the time he was 17, Battista (or 'Pinin' as he was called because he was the youngest in the family) was designing the Fiat Zero for the family firm.

With his easy-going manner, Pinin soon became head of the design office and quickly went on to be the leading force in the company.

In 1920, he travelled to the United States to judge first hand the developments in the automobile industry there. A meeting with Henry Ford in Detroit resulted in an invitation to stay in America and work for the Ford Motor Company, but Farina preferred to return to Italy. Nevertheless, he had been inspired by the size of the industry in America and by the prospects for the future. That same year, Pinin married Rosa Copasso; their first child, daughter Gianna, was born in 1922 and a son, Sergio, in 1926.

Justifiably, he wanted a bigger say in the operation of Stabilimenti Farina. When this was not forthcoming he decided to pack his bags and open his own shop, and on 30 June 1930 the doors of Carrozzeria Pinin Farina were opened for business in the city of Turin with a staff of 90, and in direct competition with his brother's company where he had begun his career 20 years earlier. His plan was to build special car bodies, but his goal was eventually to expand this operation beyond the limitations of manual craftsmen, and to transform specialised car body manufacture into an independent industry. Within a decade the Pinin Farina staff count had grown to 500 and they produced a mix of custom models as well as short production runs for manufacturers.

After the war Pinin Farina ramped up his activities as he sought to spread his expertise throughout the auto industry. Apart from some early work with Ferrari (1952), his first two big breaks came with contracts from Alfa Romeo and Peugeot in the late 1950s. Besides his unquestionable talent as a designer, the secret to Pinin Farina's long-term success can also be put down to a high degree of business nous and foresight as to where to look for new work. His understanding of the auto industry and preparedness to adapt and change with the times ensured that his company has survived to this day, unlike that of his brother, which closed its doors in 1951 after 45 years.

Battista and Rosa Farina's daughter Gianna married Renzo Carli in 1947, and a year later Carli joined Carrozzeria Pinin Farina, becoming General Manager in 1958 and later CEO in 1961 (a position he retained until 1977).

In 1961, the family name was changed by decree to Pininfarina.

From the start of his relationship with Ferrari, Pinin Farina put his son Sergio in charge of the new account. Then still in his mid-20s, the young Sergio had his hands full with the quarrelsome and sometimes abrasive Enzo Ferrari, but he eventually won over the great man with his engineering and design acumen, and his good nature, resolve, and plain honesty.

In one way, when Battista Farina handed the responsibility of nurturing the Ferrari account to his son, it signalled to Enzo Ferrari that here he was dealing with a man who would not simply buckle at his first command. While Ferrari was himself a very strong and stubborn character, it seemed that Battista Farina was cut from the same sort of cloth and was equally proud and stubborn. This was a quality that Ferrari respected and is quite likely the reason that the two men 'got on' in the way that they did, albeit through the successful attentions of Farina's diplomatic son.

It so happened that in the early 1950s Ferrari was shopping around for the design house that could satisfactorily create a style that Ferrari could call his own, and it appeared that Farina not only had the creative ability to produce the goods, but he had the strength of character that Ferrari respected. Enzo Ferrari realised that having a single or principal design house would benefit him in the long term, but the challenge for him was to find a quality company that would not be a flash in the pan, but would stay the distance and provide a stable and firm design foundation for his cars for years to come. Possessing very similar character traits, Farina and Ferrari understood each other and this was unquestionably a factor that helped to cement their relationship. At this time, the Design Director at Pinin Farina was Franco Martinengo who was responsible for all aspects of design and styling at the Turin-based design house from 1952. Over the next two decades Martinengo and his team would be responsible for, amongst many excellent Pinin Farina-designed Ferrari sports cars, the iconic 250 series, the Dino, and the mighty Daytona.

If there was a model that cemented the relationship between Ferrari and Pinin Farina it was almost certainly the 250 Europa, or the similarly-styled 375 America. These two models served to indicate to Ferrari that Pinin Farina had an understanding of what he, Ferrari, wanted, and that he had the ability to turn his ideas into saleable cars.

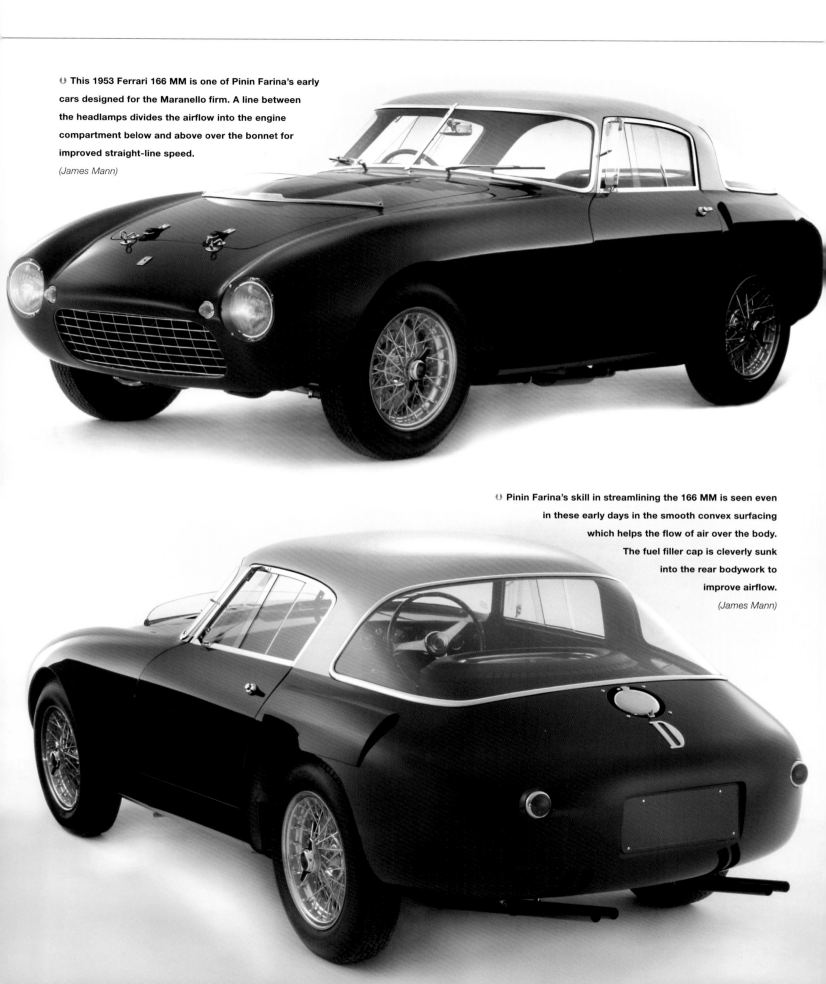

◑ This 1953 Ferrari 166 MM is one of Pinin Farina's early cars designed for the Maranello firm. A line between the headlamps divides the airflow into the engine compartment below and above over the bonnet for improved straight-line speed.

(James Mann)

◑ Pinin Farina's skill in streamlining the 166 MM is seen even in these early days in the smooth convex surfacing which helps the flow of air over the body. The fuel filler cap is cleverly sunk into the rear bodywork to improve airflow.

(James Mann)

The 1953 Pinin Farina Ferrari 166 MM is stunning from any angle, including overhead. The spare wheel can be seen through the back window, although access is rather awkwardly gained through the interior. *(James Mann)*

The stylish chrome bonnet clips have been aligned with the direction of the flow of air over the bonnet of the 166 MM, where previously they were positioned at right angles to the direction of travel. *(James Mann)*

The well-placed, stylish Perspex deflector reduces the quantity of squashed bugs on the windscreen of the Ferrari, while the bonnet vents allow hot engine air to escape. *(James Mann)*

There was concern that the tyres would tend to overheat, and this vent on the 166 MM allowed the hot air to escape.

(James Mann)

↺ 'Less is more': the
Ferrari 166 MM's styling
is brilliant in its simplicity.
(James Mann)

An example of the simple yet elegant lines for which Pinin Farina would become so well known could already be seen in the 250 Europa of 1954. First shown at the 1953 Paris Motor Show, the Vignale-bodied Europa was somewhat overshadowed by the Pinin Farina-bodied 375 America standing alongside it. As a result, Ferrari gave Pinin Farina the job of styling the remaining 250 Europas along similar lines to those of the 375 America. The Turin firm's response was to create an elegant combination of power with a slightly softer line, which went down well with those looking for a more appealing car, rather than a striking or brutish racer.

Pinin Farina followed the 250 Europa with the 250 Europa GT, which was now powered by a similar capacity, but different configuration, V12. Output was up to 220bhp, with a further increase to 240bhp two years later. The designer introduced several new styling features in a trend that was to become the hallmark of Pinin Farina's design philosophy. After the introduction of a new model, future models followed a gradual development of the original, which served to prolong the period during which the costs of chassis and drivetrain components were amortised. This process of constant upgrades also served to ensure continued model recognition by the customer and aspirational buyers, which made more sense financially than incurring the prohibitive costs associated with new model introductions every year.

In this way the 250 Europa GT was given a stylish low-level air outlet between the front wheel arch and the A-pillar, which emphasised the car's speed and aerodynamic appearance. A smaller grille made for a far more attractive front end, while neat air vents located around the rear window improved ventilation.

The glue that held Ferrari and Pinin Farina together

Breaking into the Ferrari fold was no easy task, but Pinin Farina took over the bulk of Ferrari's design work, despite Ferrari having had such a successful relationship up to then with Touring, Vignale, and others. Dale Harrow explains how two very strong and forceful characters were able to work so well together:

'If you look at the history, Pinin Farina started working with Ferrari in 1952 and I think at that time they were both very strong personalities; they were both very interested in cars but from a different perspective. And, in a sense, Enzo was more concerned with the mechanical superiority of his cars, while Farina was very concerned with the aesthetics of vehicles and how you created them.

'These two people came together and established a relationship, ensuring a fantastic opportunity to create a new product. Ferrari had been shopping around before that, but when he started working with Farina he saw their way of working was a method that they could carry on with.

'I think Ferrari probably could always have gone elsewhere, and certainly in the '80s and '90s people were coming to Ferrari and saying, "we will design cars for you", but there was a very close relationship there at a very high level, and that was absolutely essential to the way that both companies evolved.'

From the rear three-quarter view, the simple but elegant design and understated beauty of the 250 Europa can clearly be seen. *(Neill Bruce)*

The Pinin Farina-designed 1953 Ferrari 250 Europa had a long, low bonnet with a relatively high waistline, but this gave the car its sleek and fast shape. *(Neill Bruce)*

Ferrari 250 MM (1953)

The 250 MM by Pinin Farina was already showing signs of great sporting stance and poise, and this 1953 creation was a successful combination of power and elegance. The 'MM' initials were in celebration of Ferrari's victory in the 1952 Mille Miglia with the 250 S. Although the MM shared a very similar front end with the 250 S from the previous year, it had an altogether tighter and more streamlined rear section made possible by its longer wheelbase. This model hinted at greater things to come.

Up until the early 1950s, the wheels of Ferrari cars were held in place by two-eared knock-off caps. However, an American engineer, Ted Halibrand, developed the three-eared knock-off cap, which had the advantage of always having one of the ears in position for quick wheel removal by a mechanic in the pits or at the roadside. Ferrari adopted this development on its Formula 2 cars in 1952, and soon after that it was also used on its Formula 1 and road-going sports cars.

Powered by a V12 of 4.5-litre capacity, developing 300bhp, the stylish 375 America had a top speed

⊃ **Commemorating the company's victory in the 1952 Mille Miglia, the Pinin Farina-designed 1953 Ferrari 250 MM was brutally simple.** *(Geoffrey Goddard © Neill Bruce)*

◡ **The 1953 Ferrari 250 MM shows great tautness of line from this rear three-quarter angle.** *(Neill Bruce)*

⋒ Featuring the distinctive egg-crate grille, this Ferrari 250 MM is ready to do battle at the 2005 Goodwood Revival.
(Author)

⟳ Pictured in the pit garage, this 1953 Ferrari 250 MM (chassis No. 0298 MM) participated at Silverstone in celebration of Ferrari's 60th anniversary in June 2007.
(Author)

Sergio Scaglietti

Aged just 13, Sergio Scaglietti embarked upon his career in the world of metal working at the carrozzeria where his older brother was employed. The teenager, proving to be a natural, rapidly learnt the skills of the trade, and four years later his brother and a friend left to start their own coachbuilding company, taking the young but talented Sergio under their wing in the process.

They based their new company across the street from Enzo Ferrari's Auto Avio Costruzioni in Modena, and it was not long before they were repairing the early cars being raced by Ferrari in the late 1930s. This arrangement between the two companies resumed after the war, and Ferrari soon became aware of Sergio's ability. Without putting pencil to paper, his innate understanding of aerodynamics and style enabled him to fashion forms directly in aluminium, rather like a sculptor, and he took the art of automotive panelbeating to levels that few competitors could emulate.

Scaglietti's relationship with Ferrari grew to the point where he was appointed an authorised coachbuilder (1954), and he began to receive chassis direct from the factory for him to work his magic on. In due course the need grew for larger premises to accommodate the expanding activities (including bodying some of Pinin Farina's designs) that were being undertaken by the coachbuilder. With business booming throughout the 1950s the prospects looked bright, but a decade later Scaglietti's business was beset with persistent staffing troubles. When Ferrari sold his company to the Fiat Group, Scaglietti, realising that his principal source of business was about to disappear, was also prompted to sell his carrozzeria to the same buyer.

Scaglietti only retired in the mid-1980s, having continued to manage his beloved carrozzeria under Fiat's ownership until that time. During his 50 years in the automotive trade, he was responsible for some of Ferrari's most striking and accomplished competition cars, including the 500 series racers (Mondial, TR and TRC), the 250 Testa Rossa, 860 Monza, and the 250 GTO which would later become immortalised in the minds of countless sports car enthusiasts.

In recognition of Sergio Scaglietti's remarkable contribution to the industry and the important part he played in Ferrari's success, the 612 Scaglietti (2004) and the company's bespoke Carrozzeria Scaglietti customisation programme would be named after the metal worker from Modena, the birthplace of the Ferrari dream.

⊃ **This Ferrari 375 MM is fitted with a 4.5-litre Lampredi V12 engine. Bearing chassis number 0358AM, this car left the factory on 25 September 1953. The 375 differed from the 166 in that it featured a prominent bonnet scoop to help the big V12 breathe more easily, but it was still fitted with the split windscreen. This car was driven by Umberto Maglioli in the 1953 Carrera Panamericana, but did not finish.** *(Author)*

of 150mph (241kph). The 375 was devoid of any unnecessary embellishments, and was a more aesthetically pleasing combination of grace and performance. Built more as a grand tourer than a loud in-your-face sports car, the 375 America was distributed in the US by Ferrari's North American importer, Luigi Chinetti. From the impressive egg-crate grille, an elegant chrome strip swept rearwards along the sills (rocker panels) towards the attractive, pert rear end. It was a well proportioned, luxury sports car that blended Pinin Farina's graceful styling with performance and good looks, in what the designer called 'harmony' of design.

Bertone also produced designs for Ferrari and these included two special-bodied 250 GT coupés based on the 250 GT chassis, and a production car, the 308 GTB4. If Bertone had one regret it was Ferrari, but as he once said, he never tried to 'disturb' that partnership.

The 1954 Ferrari 750 Monza (chassis 0486 M) designed by Pinin Farina was the first in a long line of smaller, lightweight Ferraris from the Torino design house. This car was photographed at the Stoneleigh Historic Motorsport Show, 2005.

(Author)

Design in the 1950s and 1960s

Ferrari's first serious foray into the production car market was with the 250 (1954–62), which was developed as a road car series, and was where the initials 'GT' first appeared on Ferrari cars. This move by Ferrari resulted in an unofficial contest amongst the well-known Italian coachbuilders, from which Pinin Farina emerged as the victor. Pinin Farina (later Pininfarina) went on to style virtually all production Ferraris from the mid-1950s, and the studio's flair for creativity and innovation made an immense contribution to the marque's success. The alliance Pinin Farina formed through designing innumerable Ferrari sports cars over the years also brought enormous prestige to the Turin designer.

It is interesting to note, though, the difference in design and styling between America and Europe during the 1950s. This decade, perhaps more than any other, saw a new direction in American car design that would quite literally take that nation into another world – the world of space travel. This brave new step was in contrast to the trend in Europe, where stylists followed tradition and consolidated the sophistication and elegance for which they had become well known. That is

Keeping it simple

According to Emanuele Nicosia, Pininfarina designer between 1976 and 1985, many of the old street-racing Ferrari cars were created by means of a few sketches and the 'battilastra' (panel beaters) in Modena, such as Scaglietti and others.

'This was the real story of the great and beautiful 250 LM. Even if it is known that Pininfarina designed it, what Pininfarina did was just the interior design, even if that interior is very poor [basic] because of its racing task,' Nicosia said.

'The 250 LM was born by dressing up the great mid-engined chassis, by just covering it with metal wire sections to check any interference between body surfaces and mechanics. Then aluminium sheets were beaten and checked regularly on top of the 'wire surfaces' under the direction of the young Mauro Forghieri; it was a piece of art. After that, the body was checked and scanned (by hand of course) to produce real drawings,' he added.

not to say European designers were not exploratory, but their products tended to be less flamboyant and more aerodynamic and technically formed.

Perhaps its heritage as a nation with an extraordinary talent in art established Italy as the outstanding exception to the troubles within the coachbuilding industry after the Second World War. From the 1950s onwards the coachbuilders poured out a succession of modern, attractive designs based on popular models such as Alfa Romeo, Fiat, Lancia, and others.

Italy's growing reputation in design in general, coupled with the proliferation of imaginative car designs coming

from that country, impressed even Detroit. American car manufacturers began to incorporate some of the features of the new Italian designs in their new models, and also started to recruit Italian talent into their design studios. Ghia worked for Chrysler and Pinin Farina for Nash, for example. Italian stylists also reacted against the excesses of the more extreme American creations in the late 1950s and shifted to clean lines. It resulted in the so-called 'gran luce' (full light) style, with deep, wide windscreens and windows. This style was later picked up by other designers in the US and Europe.

'I think the way the Italians were designing cars is closely associated with the craft process, where they were making wooden models and controlling line three-dimensionally. They were making prototypes in metal of a very high quality,' explained Professor Dale Harrow, Head of Vehicle Design at the Royal College of Art in London. 'They were bringing very good artisan skills to a modern design process, but what they didn't do was to adopt wholeheartedly the kind of American clay model techniques, and I think that gave a certain quality to the finished work. The quality of line and the tension of surface is something that can only really be created through that way of working,' he said.

⌒ **The 1959 Ferrari 250 GT (SWB) is arguably one of the most perfectly designed sports racers of all time. The balance of aggression and elegance is just right.** (Author)

Tools of the trade

The 'tools' used by automotive designers in the design studios of Turin in the 1950s and 1960s were far from being 'off the shelf' items, and their curved 'sagome' (shapes), or 'balene' ('whales'), were made by the modellers themselves based on their practical knowledge and experience, and used for most of the general model scales common in Italy at the time – 1:10, 1:5, 1:1 full size (the Americans and Japanese used 1:4 instead of 1:5). According to its shape, each guide was given a name by the designers.

Originally the curved guides were made out of 'compensato' (plywood) or Masonite (chipboard), and they would reproduce the curves of the full size master line drawing using wooden sheets to check the lines against the three-dimensional model.

After refinements had been made to the three-dimensional model there would, of course, be a disparity with the original two-dimensional drawings, so the line guides fabricated by the modellers in wood were then adopted by the designers to form the lines on the revised design drawings. In time, an astute designer started to make them from transparent Perspex for use on the drawing board.

'I still use them (1:10 scale) at the beginning of a project, because they force me to check the balance and harmony of volumes and surfaces,' Emanuele Nicosia admits.

creating the wooden formers over which the metal body panels could be fabricated. This creative strength was directly connected with the post-war industrial revolution in Italy, a strength that gave them a big lead over the rest of the industry because this design method was not followed by other industrialised nations.

Italian design inspiration was frequently seen in other cars across Europe, as keen design commentator Ross Ashmore observes: 'The Mercedes-Benz 300SL Gullwing was almost certainly influenced by Italian design.' British-born Mercedes-Benz engineer responsible for

The Italian design technique developed from the way in which the subject of design was taught to students in that country at the time. The Italians had an artisan approach to teaching design in the studios, as car design was not specifically taught as a subject in Italy, and students would instead undergo classic traditional training in the field of architecture. Working as an artisan, or once qualified from university, students would be introduced into a studio and would work their way up, specialising in vehicle design, or whatever niche they chose.

Through this on-the-job training, designers could control the line of both form and shape, and they would subsequently produce very detailed tenth-scale three-dimensional drawings from their model. They would then copy the line accurately from the tenth-scale drawings in the development of the 300SL, Rudolf Uhlenhaut, was a 'man about Europe' in the 1950s and would have been influenced by the leading designs of the day.

Many of the Italian design studios preferred to use 'gesso' (a type of plaster) for making their models, rather than the clay (plasticine) that the American studios used, because it gave a finer finish. The gesso would be mixed together with the plaster, and left in a bucket until it had almost set, at which point it would be 'slapped' on to the model and scraped through the various stages very quickly with a former. 'But it made a very precise surface, a very controlled surface, unlike clay where you can keep adding and removing material. In that way, they could control the geometry and line,' explained Professor Dale Harrow.

As a nation, however, the Italians possessed a fantastic sense of style and, as Dale Harrow points out, 'There is an intrinsic quality about a lot of Italian stuff, just in terms of its styling. You don't look at Italian stuff and say "they are fantastic innovators", but what they bring is incredible refinement. It just shows what a talent hothouse Turin must have been at the time.'

⟲ The Mercedes-Benz 300SL Gullwing was a stunningly fast car, and the dual power bulges on the bonnet, the wheel-arch lips, and the strikingly beautiful air outlets just ahead of the doors all enhanced the perception of speed.
(Mercedes-Benz Archive)

♆ **The 1956 Ferrari Superfast was quite unlike any sports car that had come from Maranello before, or for that matter since, and represents a bold and innovative move by Pinin Farina.**

(Wouter Melissen)

Ferrari 410 Superamerica (SA) and 410 Superfast (1956)

'There was a language of design developing in America that was unique, unusual, and progressive, because it was all about the future, forward thinking – with the atomic car and all that sort of stuff,' Dale Harrow explained.

With talk of intercontinental jet travel and adventures into space, the 1950s could certainly be regarded as the decade of experimentation, and Harley Earl, head of GM Design, was responsible for designing some truly amazing cars that borrowed heavily from rocket and aircraft design, a trend that appealed to the American population. GM's concept cars with extravagant wings and glass domes, which looked more like spacecraft than cars, were shown all over the country. Earl's reasoning was that if he could get the American public to buy GM products by generating their enthusiasm at these shows through such futuristic models, then that was all that really mattered.

By the mid-1950s, thanks to the enthusiastic work by importer Luigi Chinetti and his small team

of distributors, North America was fast becoming Ferrari's most important export market. Through their combined activities on the track and other high-profile exploits off the track, the achievements of the NART organisation (North American Racing Team) was brought to the attention of the factory, and Ferrari took steps to recognise their valuable contribution to the development of this market. Accordingly, he cleverly named the exclusive Superamerica and Superfast models to capture the imagination of potential buyers in North America.

Not only did Ferrari introduce these strongly charged names, but those designing cars for the company took notice of the styles which appealed to the American audience. With the American public's penchant for bold and (sometimes) flashy vehicle designs, fins became bigger and aviation themes abounded, and any automobile designer wanting to make a name for himself there had to produce some winged examples in his repertoire. It was in recognition of this trend that Pinin Farina answered the call by producing the 410 Superamerica and the 410 Superfast, the latter offering some alarming styling concepts.

The 1956 Ferrari 410 Superamerica was really the model with which Ferrari acknowledged the importance of manufacturing for the North American market. A substantial sports car by any measure, it had presence and good looks, and its 4.9-litre engine was just what the Americans wanted. *(LAT)*

The 410 Superamerica was an uncomplicated design, with a simple flare splashed along the car's flanks, and hot air vents located behind the front wheel-arches. The car's wing (fender) and waistline was one continuous and uninterrupted line, devoid of any curves or shape – which served to enhance the car's length, strongly suggesting that this was a car for touring and not competition. *(LAT)*

The 410 Superamerica, the more sober of these two models, offered a very sophisticated blend of luxury and performance, but the Superfast must go down as one of the most striking Ferraris that Pinin Farina ever designed. For some, the 410 Superfast was perhaps the most 'un-Ferrari' Ferrari imaginable. While undoubtedly drawing some inspirational influence from the Bertone-designed Alfa Romeo BAT (Berlinetta Aerodinamica Tecnica) cars of 1954, the Superfast grand tourer brought together a very futuristic looking body with advanced mechanicals and running gear in an intoxicating mix of performance and elegance.

The aero-streamlining influence on the 1956 Superfast was clear, but its effectiveness was questionable. The design elements that characterise the Superfast were tasteful and elegant – such as the wings (fenders), the A-pillars and the beautifully controlled chrome. The rear wing (fender) line features a small step just at the B-pillar, a truly stylish touch. (Wouter Melissen)

The large bonnet scoop swallowed air to cool the large 5.0-litre V12 engine, while the sleek lateral outlets behind the front wheels diverted hot air away from the engine compartment. The lateral surface transition from a convex (up to the B-pillar) to a gently concave surface at the rear is quite extraordinary. (Wouter Melissen)

Debuting at the Brussels Motor Show in 1956, the 410 Superamerica was powered by a hefty 4963cc V12, producing 340bhp and capable of launching the 410 to a top speed of 220mph (354kph). By taking a leaf out of GM designer Harley Earl's book, the extraordinarily futuristic and luxurious 410 Superfast by Pinin Farina, which was launched at the Paris Salon the same year, was the result of 'thinking outside the box', and not unexpected for this period.

The front end was an extremely modern and strong example of Pinin Farina's work in which the lower profile bonnet line was made possible by the wide, elliptical grille. This lower bonnet gave the car a strong and sleek aerodynamic line, which was visually enhanced by jet-like air vents on the flanks just behind the wheel-arches which allowed hot air to escape from the engine bay. High-level vents on the B-pillar just behind the door windows ensured the free flow of air through the cabin.

Drawing further inspiration from the aerodynamic efficiency of the aircraft world, the rear flanks rose into prominent but stylish wings that several American automotive designers, such as Harley Earl, were using at the time to great effect in the US.

Faired-in headlamps and forward protruding projectile-like indicators gave the 410 Superfast a distinctive space-age look, while an attractive low-level chrome strip along the car's flanks enhanced the two-tone paint scheme applied to this model. The rear wheels were half concealed with wheel covers, adding to the perception of fluidity and speed, while also giving the 410 Superfast a more streamlined appearance. Commenting on the complex convex/concave surface transition in the rear flank, Dale Harrow said, 'It's beautifully done. That surface development is incredibly difficult to do, to go from the convex to the concave surface without getting a curious kind of highlight line.'

Although the Superfast styling was not widely accepted in Europe, it had an international flavour to it because of the liberal, contemporary thinking at the time. As Dale Harrow points out, 'America was perceived as being the technological, emerging centre of everything,' so the unusual Ferrari design was hailed as a successful Italian interpretation of American flair and passion. It would have been unthinkable to try selling a European car into the American market at that time that didn't sport tail fins of some description, and which did not draw some influence from the age of jet travel.

This extravagant styling said, 'let's do it anyway,' and it seemed to throw all caution to the wind because, although they were attractive, the fins and sweeping bodywork were of little aerodynamic value. 'It's definitely streamlined styling rather than aero styling. It's unapologetic, really. They must have worked incredibly closely with Ferrari on the packaging of this model,' suggested Dale Harrow. In fact, the model played host to more innovative design firsts than any Ferrari model before, but it did not detract from the car's striking good looks. Progressive design is always about pushing the boundaries and trying something new, but the 410 Superfast must have been quite a challenge for Farina, requiring rather more than the usual amount of discussion and persuasion to get acceptance in Maranello. Having made the decision to go that route, however, they did it very well and, in terms of development, one can see within the vehicle a refinement that was not seen in American cars of that period.

Some thirty 410 Superamerica bodies were produced by Boano and Ghia. Felice Mario Boano is probably one of Italy's most underrated designers. He took over the ailing Ghia design house with a friend upon Ghia's sudden death in 1944, but after some years he left Ghia to work under his own name. Boano's designs showed obvious Italian style but with influences of the contemporary American automobiles of the time. The 410 Superamerica and a special 375 MM were the last Ferraris to be bodied by Ghia.

It is very much about craftsmanship. Every element that is on there is beautiful. You look at this and you could take almost any component off and it would be a thing of beauty in its own right.
(Wouter Melissen)

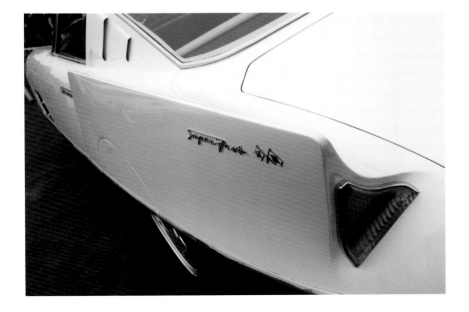

Ferrari 250 GT Tour de France (1956)

The word 'legendary' is an oft-overused adjective when describing significant road or race cars, but in the case of the 250 GT, Ferrari's longest-lived road/race series, its use is fully justified. Destined to be a winner from the outset, this sports car was lifted to prominence when Alfonso de Portago drove one of the first examples to victory in the 1956 Tour de France. This early victory marked the beginning of Ferrari's long-running dominance in GT racing with its 3-litre sports cars. Although the 250 GT Berlinetta was to become known as the 'Tour de France', this informal reference was never officially used by the factory as a model name.

Created and built by Scaglietti, the all-aluminium bodied 250 GT took many design cues from the 410 Superamerica and Superfast, from the car's elliptical grille and faired-in headlamps, to the well-formed but strong rear end. This sports car's aggressive looks are enhanced by the leading edge of the roof line, which appears to creep slightly into the windscreen space creating the effect of a creased brow and giving the car a 'focused' look, a perception which is also enhanced by the small side windows.

It was powered by the smaller of the two 12-cylinder units developed by Ferrari at the time, the renowned Colombo 3-litre V12 that generated a healthy 240bhp. Following the disaster at the 1955 Le Mans 24-Hour, a 3-litre limit had been laid down by the sporting authorities in an effort to reduce racing speeds and prevent the recurrence of such an incident.

Shortened to simply the 'TdF', the 250 GT's basic design was extremely effective and proved to be one of Ferrari's most successful sports racing cars. The Milanese design house, Zagato (SZ Design S.R.L.), also bodied a couple of 250 GTs that featured a distinctive 'double bubble' roof profile.

Small but regular upgrades distinguished the various 250 GT models, such as sliding or wind-up windows, cowled, covered or plain headlights, and varying grille treatments, all of which gave the car quite a different appearance from year to year. Louvres located in the rear roof pillar provided much-improved cockpit ventilation.

The formidable 250 GT TdF was one of the last long-wheelbase 250s (2,600mm/102½in), being replaced by the 250 GT SWB (2,400mm/94½in) in 1959.

The 1956 Ferrari 250 GT Competizione has a very different rear end from its later siblings, as there is no boot, its place being taken by a racing fuel tank (note the fuel filler in the centre of the rear panel). The rear end is also more rounded and compact and is devoid of fins as in the later model. *(Neill Bruce)*

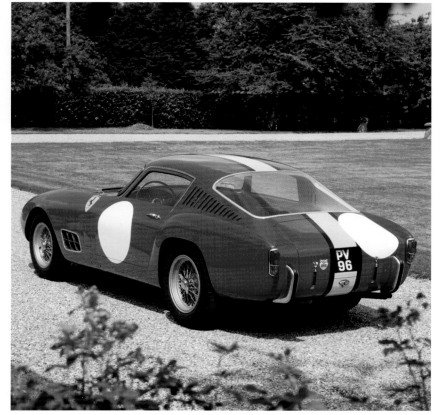

The difference between this 1957 250 TdF and the other two cars pictured here is that the air vent located behind the doors consists of 14 slats – the later car had just a single vent, while the earlier car had none. Driven by Olivier Gendebien and Jacques Washer, this works Ferrari 250 TdF (chassis 0677) finished third in 1957 Mille Miglia. *(Neill Bruce)*

⋂ The 1958 model 250 GT Tour de France, the last of this series, featured a bonnet scoop and covered-in headlamps which were set slightly further back in the wings (fenders) than in the 1956 model. *(Neill Bruce)*

⊃ Sold new to Cuban racing driver 'Alfonsito' Alfonso Gomez-Mena in February 1959, this late model 250 GT TdF (chassis 1035GT) was driven by the Cuban in the Tour de France.

(Neill Bruce)

The 250 GT LWB Tour de France is a single-louvre model from 1959, featuring uncovered headlamps and a smaller radiator grille with a declining bow-shaped body line between the front headlamps. (*Author*)

This 1958 model 250 GT LWB Tour de France is a single-louvre model featuring covered headlamps and a smaller radiator grille with an inclining bow-shaped body line between the front headlamps. (*Author*)

Yet another example of the 250 GT LWB Tour de France, this time a 14-louvre model featuring a different headlamp design. This No. 56 car (0607 GT) is a 1957 model and took part in that year's Mille Miglia. (*Author*)

↑↻ The Cartier 'Style et Luxe' is possibly one of the world's most coveted car design competitions. A concours d'élégance extraordinaire, it is a celebration of the beautiful, the imaginative, and the innovative in automotive design. Featured at the Goodwood Festival of Speed's 2007 'Style et Luxe', a cherished bastion of artistry and good taste, was this 1957 version of Ferrari's 250 GT Tour de France. *(Author)*

The demise of the 250 GT LWB TdF was followed in 1959 by the 250 GT LWB Interim, a model which more than hinted at the shape of the 250 GT SWB which was to succeed the TdF, but was still built on the 2,600mm (102½in) chassis.

One of the great success stories of the 3-litre V12-engined 250 series built between 1953 and 1964 is the flexibility of these great cars, since their owners could just as easily race them as use them for everyday driving. This duality of use makes the 250 series one of the absolute all-time greatest legends of the road or track. Is it any wonder, then, that its successor in 1959, the 250 GT SWB, was just as successful in competition and every bit as good in terms of being a design success?

A number of cabriolets were produced in the 250 GT series, which served to further establish the range as a formidable part of the Ferrari stable. The 250 GT Cabriolet was first introduced in March 1957 at the Geneva Motor Show and was powered by the potent 2953cc V12 engine. The pre-production model by Pinin Farina was styled with graceful yet muscular lines, borrowing some design cues from the Tour de France and the 410 Superamerica (initially this model used the 2,600mm/102½in long-wheelbase chassis), such as the faired-in headlamps and the hot air extraction vents on the lower wings (fenders). The Turin designer succeeded in combining both flat and curved surfaces in this elegant and purposeful body.

⊃ It is difficult to call any Ferrari 'plain', but perhaps the 1959 Ferrari 250 GT Cabriolet comes fairly close. Pinin Farina's design for this model was referred to as 'restrained' as it had little in the way of external embellishments. *(James Mann)*

⋂ Some confusion existed in identifying the 250 GT Cabriolet and Spyder models, and Pinin Farina sought to clarify this by aligning the Cabriolet more closely with the Coupé. The Spyder featured recessed headlamps, and it retained the flank-mounted engine hot air vents which this model, a 1960 250 GT Cabriolet Series II, had lost. *(Neill Bruce)*

In December 1960, the 250 GT California was introduced at the behest of John von Neumann, the American West Coast distributor, who had done much to bolster the Porsche marque in the same lucrative market. Von Neumann's clientele included many of Hollywood's film stars who were eager to be seen in the best and most stylish sports cars from Italy.

Designed by Pinin Farina and styled by Scaglietti, the California was built on a shorter 2,400mm (94½in) wheelbase and was fitted with the more powerful (280bhp) V12 Tour de France engine of the same 3-litre capacity. Scaglietti took the best points of the GT Cabriolet, making the California even more modern and stylish than before – perfect for cruising the boulevards of California during those balmy summer evenings.

◯ Ferrari's SWB California (2,400mm), which must rank as one of Ferrari's most attractive and sporting cabriolets, was introduced at the 1960 Geneva Motor Show. This 1962 model is fitted with a removable hardtop. *(Neill Bruce)*

⊃ Count Giovanni Volpi di Misurata started a racing team, Scuderia Serenissima, and quickly became one of Ferrari's best customers. This 1959 250 LWB California (chassis 1459 GT with 250 TR engine) was one of his cars, but following the great walkout at the end of October 1961, Volpi felt the wrath of Enzo Ferrari, who refused to sell him the two 250 GTOs he requested. Volpi went on to provide the financing for the ATS race organisation, staffed by the dissident ex-Ferrari personnel. *(Neill Bruce)*

↻ Borrani wire wheels have long been used on Ferrari road and race cars. Founded in 1922, the Borrani wire wheel was originally manufactured in Italy under licence from the English firm Rudge Whitworth. The stylish wheels on this 250 LWB California are complemented by the elegant engine exit vents and understated chrome sill (rocker) strip. *(Neill Bruce)*

⋔ Several styling features that appeared on the 250 LWB California were carried over from the 250 GT TdF, such as the oval grille with lights, the recessed and faired-in headlamps, and bonnet scoop. *(Neill Bruce)*

⋔ Without any chrome bumpers, this model's more pronounced wings gave the car a menacingly sporty appearance. Bodied by Scaglietti, the California was both elegant and powerful. *(Neill Bruce)*

⟳ No matter what angle it is viewed from, the 250 LWB California is stunning to look at. *(Neill Bruce)*

⋒ Based on the longer 2,600mm (102¼in) wheelbase, this Ferrari 250 GT Ellena Coupé was one of the 50 produced by Ezio Ellena, son-in-law to the great Mario Felice Boano who had taken over the production of the second series 250 GTs from Pinin Farina.

(James Mann)

⋐ This 250 GT Ellena Coupé, 25th of just 50 built, was sold new in May 1958. An unusual feature on this car is the air scoop on the bonnet, as most of the Boano 250s had flat bonnets.

(James Mann)

With the intention of producing the 250 in greater numbers, the second series GT Cabriolet was introduced at the 1959 Paris Motor Show, resulting in 200 examples being built during the car's three-year production run. Both comfort and power were increased, while the styling was somewhat simplified by the removal of the side vents, and rather ordinary chrome headlamp surrounds replaced the smooth Perspex covers.

The introduction of the 250 GT Coupé revived a model first launched in 1954, the 250 Europa GT. Produced almost on an industrial level (for Ferrari anyway), 335 cars were built in just two years between 1958 and 1960, pushing the Maranello factory into new territory in terms of production capability. Characterised by simplicity in both line and form, the long-wheelbase (2,600mm) 250 GT Coupé was, nevertheless, stylish and imposing and almost devoid of any surplus features or styling elements. This model was destined to be a grand tourer with no pretensions at competition, and was therefore produced with comfort in mind.

Ferrari 250 GT SWB

'There was something very nice going on in Italy at that time. Look at Lancia, there was some beautiful engineering and refinement there. In a sense, they brought together the idea of a whole design – the engineering, the bodywork, and everything else,' Dale Harrow says.

Without any doubt, the 250 GT sports coupé designed by Pinin Farina and built by Scaglietti on the short-wheelbase (2,400mm) chassis is the car on which Ferrari's sporting prowess would be based for the next decade. This model is also recognised as one of the forerunners of the true modern-day coupé sports car. Better known as the 250 SWB, this model was introduced at the 1959 Paris Motor Show and used the same basic 2953cc V12 engine, but with some modifications. In 280bhp race trim, the 250 SWB wrote the company into the history books.

Quite different from the 250 Tour de France, this gracefully designed road/race car from the pen of Rabbone is arguably the most handsome and brutish Ferrari sports car ever made. Fitted with disc brakes on all four wheels, this model was a formidable force during its first year as a homologated racer. In 1960, four 250 SWB cars occupied fourth to seventh overall

◑ Although the 250 GT Competizione is considered to be the forefather of the 250 sports car range, it was based on the long 2,600mm (102¼in) wheelbase. In 1959, the 250 GT SWB was introduced, and with its shorter 2,400mm (94½in) wheelbase, it proceeded to rewrite sports car racing history. This example above, chassis 1993 GT, was the first car sold in the UK by Maranello Concessionaires Ltd. *(Neill Bruce)*

◑ This rear three-quarter photo highlights what a complete racer the 250 GT SWB was, with its beautifully simple lines, tight rump, and athletic stance. *(Neill Bruce)*

↺ Scaglietti's attention to detail was, as always, superb. The forward sloping engine air exit vent enhanced the perception of speed on this 1960 250 SWB. *(Neill Bruce)*

↪ Quad exhaust outlets and round rear lights became a hallmark of Ferrari's 250-series racers in the 1960s. *(Neill Bruce)*

placings in the Le Mans 24-Hours, while other notable achievements included wins in the Tour de France and the Intereuropa Cup at Monza in 1960, as well as the Tourist Trophy at Goodwood in 1961 in the capable hands of Stirling Moss.

Sharing some of the front-end design elements with the 250 TdF, the 250 SWB is that perfect combination of both power and grace, which characterised sports car design in the late 1950s and early 1960s. Featuring a prominently positioned central bonnet air scoop and wide grille similar to that of the California, the body tapered back to the shapely rump and fastback rear windscreen. The car's relatively low windscreen and roof height, with its tastefully styled greenhouse, was typical of many sports cars of the day, but no other manufacturer got the balance of form and function quite as beautifully correct as Pinin Farina did with this model. The 1961 model was equipped with an exit vent mounted in the roof at the centre rear, whereas earlier cars did not have this. The neat and tight rear end was punctuated with a pair of twin-stacked round lights and four menacing exhaust outlets.

A wheelbase of 2,400mm (94½in) is considered the ideal length for a race car of this era, allowing good cornering characteristics (the shorter, the better) and straight-line stability (the longer, the better). If there was a chink in the armour of the 250 SWB, it was the short nose of the car that hampered its top speed on long straights like the Mulsanne at Le Mans. A

distinguishing feature of the earlier 250s was a kink at the top rear edge of the side windows; this was straightened out on later models. If anything, this kink enhanced the appeal of the earlier cars and showed the creative hand of its designer.

The aluminium-bodied 250 GT LWB TdF weighed in at 1,145kg, while its successor, the steel-bodied 250 GT SWB, topped the scales at 1,100kg. The aluminium-bodied SWB weighed a mere 960kg, which partly accounted for the significant increase in top speed from 155mph (250kph) to 166mph (268kph).

In the opinion of Sergio Farina, the 250 SWB was a perfect example of how one can achieve great expressive strength with simplicity and purity of lines, and harmony of proportion. In a company press release, he said, 'This is why the 250 SWB is a timeless car, as beautiful today as it was then. The distance between the 250 SWB and its competitors is enormous.'

The axiom 'all other cars seem meaningless compared to her' would seem to be an appropriate phrase to describe the 250 SWB. Somehow, Pinin Farina did a particularly good job of basically keeping it simple, and simple cars generally tend to look better than over-designed cars. Asked whether beauty and function can co-exist, Nick Mason replied, 'When looking at cars of the '50s and '60s, no one had got too involved in wind tunnels, so all those sort of slats and wings were not really an issue. Basically, it was a case of "if it looks right, it is right".'

Ferrari sports cars have long been the favourites of film stars and music greats. This 1960 Ferrari 250 GT SWB (chassis 2335 GT) was once owned by the famous guitarist Eric Clapton. *(Neill Bruce)*

A 1962 steel-bodied 250 GT SWB. *(Neill Bruce)*

Photographed at the Brooklands Auto Italia Day in 2005, this close-up of a Ferrari 250 SWB shows the detail of the rear wing (fender) air vent. *(Author)*

Photographed in the pre-race garage at Silverstone, this 250 GT SWB awaits its moment on the track on the occasion of Ferrari's 60th anniversary at the Northampton circuit on 10 June 2007. *(Author)*

Beauty and the beast
– PART 1

An Italian car is the type of car you would like to marry, but a German car is like a reliable friend. While you can be passionate about Italian design, you won't necessarily want to marry your friend.

– ROSS ASHMORE
Art and design critic

Ferrari in the early 1960s

Many of the influences in the design evolution of Ferraris throughout the 1960s came from the 1956 Superfast. Although this model is best known for its unusual fins and 'pillarless' windscreen, it is the frontal treatment of the car that lived on in many of the 1960s models.

In 1961 the family name of Farina was changed by decree to Pininfarina. That same year, aged 68, Battista Pininfarina, having worked for over 50 years, decided to retire, and he handed over the running of the company to his son Sergio and his son-in-law Renzo Carli.

About one month before his death on 3 April 1966, Pininfarina appeared in public, along with the President of the Republic, at the inauguration of the Pininfarina Studies and Research Centre.

During his lifetime Pininfarina received many honours and tributes, including the Légion d'Honneur from General de Gaulle, and he was made an honorary member of the Royal Society of Arts, a Fellow Royal Designer for Industry, and honorary member of the Engineer and Architect Society of Turin.

Pininfarina's strength stemmed from their independence in the market, something that was recognised by many manufacturers in Italy and the rest of Europe, and something that, to their benefit, the company protected passionately, leading to a total sale of almost 2.9 million vehicles (by 2009) to more than 150 world markets.

With the growth of prosperity in North America in the early 1960s, Ferrari was well placed through Pininfarina's innovative and stylish designs to take advantage of the increasing interest in his products, which led to the emergence of two distinctive product lines. The worldwide success of Ferrari cars on the track undoubtedly fuelled the desire among the wealthy to buy into this exclusive club, and Pininfarina produced some of his most memorable work during this period.

250 GTE 2+2 (1960)

Perhaps one of the more underrated V12 Ferraris of the 1960s, the 250 GTE offered acceptable 2+2 seating and the usual 3-litre performance. Launched at the 1960 Paris Motor Show, this model, which used the longer 2,600mm (102½in) wheelbase chassis as the coupé model, was able to accommodate the extra two passengers by moving the engine forward by 20cm

⮌ Described as being 'elegantly sober' in its styling, the 1961/62 Ferrari 250 GT 2+2 nevertheless offered real presence on the road.

(Author)

⮎ The 1962 Ferrari 250 GTE 2+2 was devoid of any decorative or chromed styling features, which left the flanks somewhat unprotected.

(Neill Bruce)

⮎ A rather simple air vent in the front wings (fenders) allowed hot engine air to escape on this 250 GTE 2+2. *(Neill Bruce)*

(about 8in) at the expense of the car's handling, which now understeered marginally. However, the owner of such a car was less likely to want to drive it on the limit to the same extent as the owner of a similar two-seater GT vehicle.

Ferrari 250 GTO (1962)

'There is something fantastically sexy about it [the 250 GTO], you know, it spells out what it does and what it is going to do. For me, it is also one of the most beautiful cars ever made. But I would have to say that, because I have got one,' confesses Nick Mason with a smile.

Ferrari's desire was to be competitive on the European circuits as well as the American tracks in the sports car racing arena, not just in Formula 1, and this resulted in some extremely beautiful but functional sports car designs that were also very aerodynamic.

As always happens in industry, companies watch the opposition, and with the Jaguar D-type's dominance

⊙ A rather special 1960 Ferrari 250 GT Nembo Spyder pictured amongst other Maranello classics at the March Motor Works garage, Goodwood Revival. (*Author*)

of the late 1950s still fresh in the minds of the Ferrari engineers, they decided that a response would be urgently needed when the new E-type was unveiled in Geneva in 1961. It was Ferrari Sales Manager, Girolamo Gardini, who returned to Maranello after the Geneva Motor Show with the news that Jaguar had just unveiled a sports car that was clearly going to be a threat to them on the race tracks for some time to come.

Having successfully accomplished the not insignificant job of convincing 'Il Commendatore' of the seriousness of the threat to the company, Experimental Sports Car Development Chief Giotto Bizzarrini was charged with heading a project task force to come up with a suitable challenger to the E-type. However, as Emanuele Nicosia recalls, 'The 250 GTO genesis is quite strange … the first prototype was designed by Bizzarrini but … it was really ugly and it wasn't accepted by Enzo. Then, starting from the Bizzarrini proposal, Scaglietti did it under the great direction of Mauro [Forghieri]. All racing cars or racing versions were designed in Maranello under the direction of Mauro.'

Ferrari's response was the 250 Gran Turismo Omologata (GTO) based on the short-wheelbase chassis (2,400mm), which, without doubt, has immortalised Ferrari sports cars in the minds of most followers around the world. The car was tested by Stirling Moss and was introduced to the press in February 1962. It had the

⋂ **The front three-quarter view of this 1962 Ferrari 250 GTO (chassis 4115 GT) highlights the sleek and low lines of this great sports racer.** *(Neill Bruce)*

⋃ **The obvious calm that surrounds the 250 GTO belies its awesome power. From the rear, the wonderfully sensuous and powerful haunches give this car superb poise.** *(Neill Bruce)*

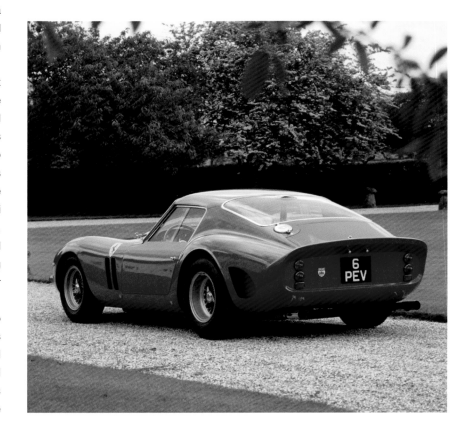

250 GT SWB, which had already been homologated by the FIA, the required quantity had therefore been met. All were built to race, but they were theoretically usable on the street by virtue of the sports-racing rules that required road versions of competition cars. It was this regulation, in fact, that gave rise to the car's name: Gran Turismo Omologato (Italian for 'Grand Touring Homologated'), in essence a GT car homologated for racing. In this way he slipped this limited-production purpose-built competition coupé into a class meant for volume-built sports cars. The result was slaughter, as the 250 GTO racked up one victory after another.

The aluminium body is taut and finely sculptured over the tubular steel chassis, while the power bulge in the bonnet accommodates six 38DCN Weber carburettors which sit atop the glorious 3-litre V12 engine. 'The three removable flaps in the nose of the 250 GTO were for engine cooling but, as Mauro said, they were not that useful and did not benefit the engine at all. They decided not to disturb aerodynamics on the following version which had a clean bonnet … it is amazing that those flaps became one of 250 GTO's icons, even though they did not work at all,' recalled Nicosia.

The engine was moved back behind the front axle, which improved weight balance for better handling and also created a lower, more aerodynamic bonnet line. A new steeply-raked windscreen and a hand-formed fastback completed the silhouette.

To all intents and purposes, the 250 GTO was an orthodox, some might say conservative, evolution of the 250 GT SWB, and the car was intended to achieve race victories – any thoughts of looking beautiful were secondary. Chief engineer Giotto Bizzarrini took the chassis from the 250 GT SWB, modified it with smaller tubes for lighter weight and additional bracing for extra stiffness, and fitted the 3.0-litre V12 engine from the ultra-successful 250 Testa Rossa.

Ironically, the 250 GTO was created during turbulent times at the Maranello factory, as a dispute in November 1961 between Sales Manager Girolamo Gardini and Enzo Ferrari resulted in Gardini's dismissal. Gardini's supporters, who included Manager Romolo Tavoni, Chief Engineer Carlo Chiti, Experimental Sports Car Development Chief Giotto Bizzarrini, and several other senior figures, were all ousted from Ferrari. This mass dismissal of key employees, at a crucial stage in the factory's programme, proved to be a huge loss for Ferrari.

◖ Doing what a 250 GTO does best, racing! Here a 1963 Ferrari 250 GTO leads an arch-rival, a Shelby Cobra, at the Goodwood Revival meeting in 2006. *(Author)*

◗ The unusual light green colour of this 250 GTO (chassis 3505 GT) identifies it as the winner of the 1962 Tourist Trophy in the hands of Innes Ireland. The large exit vents behind the rear wheels allow hot air to escape from the brakes, and prevent the tyres from overheating. *(Neill Bruce)*

tensed haunches of a cat ready to pounce, the muscular and powerful lines of an athlete, and the searching snout of a bird of prey – this had to be one of the most evocative car shapes ever created. It won the hearts and minds of most motoring enthusiasts and the 250 GTO has gone on to become one of the most recognisable sports car shapes in the world.

All told, just 39 examples of the GTO were produced, although the FIA required 100 examples to be made in order to qualify for homologation purposes. Ferrari successfully argued that as the GTO was just a modified

After this, development of the 250 GTO was handed over to new engineer Mauro Forghieri, who worked with Sergio Scaglietti on the body. Unlike most other Ferraris of the day, the 250 GTO was not designed by a specific individual or design house. Whilst a proven feature in its racing cars, this was the first combination road/race model to sport a discreet up-turned duck tail.

'There was some beautiful engineering and refinement happening in Italy at that time. With many of their cars, you had the sense that they got together the idea of a whole design, the engineering, the bodywork, and everything else,' observed Dale Harrow.

The 250 GTO was the most coveted of all sports cars. It is a car that any designer worth his salt might say, 'I wish I had designed that'.

Nick Mason says, 'I always maintain it to be one of the best cars ever made, and it is because it will do so many things well and, you know, no car can do everything. The GTO is a racing car, but you can run it in a long distance rally and live with it. You can use it on the road. It's that balance, it is not so powerful that the brakes are completely defeated by it, it is that balance of power against braking against handling, and that really is what makes it a great car at the end of the day.'

⏶ **A profile shot of the 1963 250 GTO which shows the unrivalled proportions of this sports racer. A long bonnet/ short rear layout is just perfect as the engine can be located in a mid-front position giving the car excellent balance. This car (chassis 4293 GT) finished first in the Spa 500km (Willy Mairesse) where Ferraris filled the top five places, the first three being GTOs. This same car then finished second at Le Mans (Jean Blaton/Gerard Langlois von Ophem) while two further GTOs finished 4th and 6th in 1963.** *(Neill Bruce)*

⏷ **Although the three air intakes in the bonnet have become synonymous with Ferrari 250 GTO styling, they had little cooling effect.** *(Author)*

Ferrari 330 LMB (1963)

Only four of these 330 LMB sports racers, the 250 GTO's big sister, were built by Scaglietti, and they featured a 4-litre V12 engine. Seemingly an amalgamation of styles, the 330 appeared to have the tapered front of the 250 GTO and the rear end of the 250 GTL, although with a more aggressive rear lip akin to that of the GTO.

Built on a 2,500mm (98½in) wheelbase, this was the result of an earlier experiment carried out on a lengthened 250 GTO. Other GTO similarities included the front wing slats with matching outlets on the rear wings (fenders), while high rear wheel-arch vents allowed cooling for the tyres and additional rear wheel travel. Despite the car's awesome potential – it developed 400bhp and had a top speed of 174mph (280kph) – the 330 LMB did not enjoy as illustrious a sporting career as the 250 GTO did.

↷ The Ferrari 330 LMB featured a front end that was almost identical to the 250 GTO. This 1963 model was photographed in the pre-race paddock at the Goodwood Revival meeting in 2006. *(Author)*

↻ In its element – the Ferrari 330 LMB leads a group of racers through the Esses at Goodwood. *(Author)*

250 Gran Turismo Lusso (1963)

In Sergio Pininfarina's view, Ferrari reached the peak of elegance with the Berlinetta Lusso. Together with a bigger greenhouse (more glass), the mobility and purity of its lines gave the 250 GT Lusso the appearance of lightness not seen in earlier models. However, under this refined, less aggressive exterior lurked the 'character of a tiger' according to Pininfarina.

The 250 GT Lusso (or GTL) was a deviation from contemporary Ferrari trends at that time. The auxiliary lamps, previously located within the confines of the grille, were moved outwards and stylishly incorporated in the bodywork beneath the main headlamps. The simplicity of this car's design is its strongest attribute – there are no aggressive or conflicting lines.

This model represents an excellent example of the Berlinetta body style, the Italian interpretation of the French Berline form, a four-door saloon (sedan). The 'etta' suffix refers to a small form of this body style, and in the Italian context, it typically refers to a small post-war, two-door, closed saloon (sedan) or coupé with a fastback or sloping rear end. Quite usually, when referring to the Berlinetta body form, as produced by manufacturers such as Alfa Romeo, Fiat, and Ferrari, one is talking about sports cars or fast performance versions of saloon (sedan) models.

Launched at the 1962 Paris Motor Show, the Berlinetta Lusso (luxury) left one in no doubt that this Ferrari was created with comfort in mind. Body-

⌒ The rear styling of Ferrari's 250 GT Berlinetta Lusso already hinted at the 275 GTB, which was introduced the following year. *(Neill Bruce)*

↻ The 250 GTL's beautifully flowing lines all start with the low and shark-like front end. This car was photographed at the Goodwood Revival meeting in 2006. *(Author)*

hugging leather bucket seats kept occupants firmly in place, while the dashboard was something of a departure from tradition. Located centrally were the large twin rev-counter and speedo dials, while a grouping of four smaller dials (oil pressure and temperature, water temperature and fuel) were directly ahead of the driver.

Sporting a lower and more streamlined nose section, a step forward from the 250 SWB but still with some similarities, the 250 GTL embraced an altogether more sleek and, therefore, lower line. For the first time, Ferrari's road cars displayed large round tail lights, a trend that was to continue through many future models and can even be seen in the 599 GTB and F430 cars today.

Ferrari 500 Superfast (1964)

○ **The 500 Superfast has great presence, and is seen at its best from this angle. The car looks truly regal and sporting.**

(James Mann)

The 400 Superamerica and Superfast II of 1960 were entirely different from those models of the same name produced four years earlier. The 1956 Superamerica featured a 4.9-litre V12 engine and was almost brutish-looking with a more squared off front and back end, while the later car was fitted with a 3.9-litre V12.

The Superamerica of 1960 followed an entirely different theme from its predecessor and was aerodynamically styled, from its thin, tapered front end to the equally thin and wedge-shaped tail section. There was no doubt that Farina was appealing to an elite subset, even within the exclusive Ferrari market.

With the introduction in 1964 of the 500 Superfast, Pininfarina took this style a step further by creating a more pleasing front end, but the rear view of this touring model appears rushed, or unfinished.

○ **The rear view of the Ferrari 500 Superfast unfortunately does not live up to its superbly-styled front. Although the tapered back end may be aerodynamically efficient, and the 500 was regarded as a 'breakaway' design, it is almost as though this aspect was left to last, and the designer ran out of time.** *(James Mann)*

The mighty 5-litre developed 400bhp and, aided by a super-sleek design, could push the Superfast to a top speed of 174mph (280kph). Careful detailing ensured that the sports tourer was a superb example of understated elegance. *(James Mann)*

The rear lights of the 500 Superfast are uncharacteristically at odds with the car's otherwise superb flowing lines. *(Author)*

Ferrari 250 GTO/64

Derived as the successor to the immortal 250 GTO of 1962, the much 'chunkier' looking 250 GTO/64 seemed to lose its way somewhat. Not intended for road use, the aggressive looking 250 GTO/64 compared exactly with the technical spec of its predecessor.

The body appeared far larger than it actually was because the '64' was shorter but wider than the model it replaced. This model's broad appearance was enhanced by its lower roofline, which was more than 100mm (4in) lower than the 1962 car. This was achieved by further inclining the front windscreen, but the most dramatic treatment was reserved for the car's rear end.

Cleverly, the much shorter, chopped-off tail gave the perception of a long bonnet despite the car actually being almost 200mm (8in) shorter overall. However, the rear window was framed by stubby buttresses that formed a kind of tunnel around the glass which served to add strength to the body structure. Although it is difficult to imagine that this model was the direct descendant of the original GTO, widely regarded as one of the most beautiful sports cars ever made, the overall design of the GTO/64 was nevertheless very striking and purposeful.

⌒ Many Ferrari enthusiasts regard the Ferrari 275 GTB as one of the best sports cars to come from the Maranello factory. This model shows the superb balance and stance of this sports racer. *(Neill Bruce)*

↻ Gently flowing lines ensured the 275 GTB was pleasing from any angle. The long bonnet hid the larger 3.3-litre V12 power plant. *(Neill Bruce)*

Ferrari 275 GTB and GTS

Introduced at the 1964 Paris Motor Show, the Ferrari 275 GTB (Berlinetta), which replaced the 250 GTL, was perhaps the advent of the big-engined, big-presence, and powerful-looking Grand Touring models from Maranello.

The 275 GTB, styled by Aldo Bravarone in the Pininfarina studio, announced to the world that Ferrari had intentions – big intentions – of retaining their position as the manufacturers of the finest, most powerful sports cars in the world. Now boasting a 3.3-litre V12 engine producing 280bhp, the 275 GTB looked like it could beat just about anything on the road. In competition, though, it did little, managing just a class win and eighth overall in the 1966 Le Mans 24-Hours.

From its sleek and perfectly-formed oval grille to the short, cropped tail, the 275 was everything a sports car lover could want. With hindsight, this model was in fact the forefather of, and in no small measure the inspiration for, future front-engined giant killers from Maranello, such as the 330 GTC and the 365 GTB (Daytona).

There are those who feel that the 275 GTB is one of the best-looking Ferrari coupés ever made, and they have a very strong case. However, there are also those who feel that the car's styling balance is upset by its extremely long bonnet. Whichever camp you fall into, one cannot dispute that the 275 certainly had presence, thanks to its powerful and muscular front and rear wings (fenders). The rise and fall of the wing (fender) line mimic the muscles of a well-developed body-builder, while the car's predatory abilities are further enhanced by the shark-like gills on the front flanks, which allowed the mighty 3.3-litre V12 to breathe.

'I really love the 275 GTB, a masterpiece of proportion, volume, balance, personality, and power. It imparts the feeling of an emotional creature even at rest in the garage,' confessed Nicosia.

Built on the 2,400mm (94½in) short wheelbase, the 275 represented several technical advances for the company, not least of which was the increased capacity engine. For the first time on a road-going Ferrari, the 275 boasted independent suspension on all four wheels, while the gearbox was mounted in the rear together with the differential for improved all-round balance, a first for road-going Ferraris. Another break in tradition came in 1966 with solid alloy wheel rims replacing the wire wheels.

⋂ **This high front angle emphasises the proportion of the 275 GTB's substantial bonnet, a design aspect intended to convey an overwhelming image of power. The power bulge down the centre indicates the later four-cam engine.**

(James Mann)

⊃ **A simple flat 'Kamm' tail is what most other motorists would see of the 275 GTB on the road.**

(Neill Bruce)

⌒ This 1966 Series II model had its nose extended to reduce front-end lift at speed. *(Neill Bruce)*

⟳ The strong proportions of the Ferrari 275 GTB/4 can be seen in this atmospheric black-and-white photo taken in London.
(Motor Industry Archives)

⟳ The single round rear lights on the 275 GTB (1964) would become a hallmark of Ferrari's front-engined sports cars, and are still used by them today. *(Author)*

➲ The Ferrari 275 GTS was introduced at the 1964 Paris Motor Show at the same time as the GTB, but the two models looked very different from each other. *(James Mann)*

◡ Confusingly, Ferrari's 275 GTS and GTB models shared the same chassis and mechanicals, but the Spyder adopted the rear end of the 330 2+2, suitably modified for the open car. This silver 1965 275 GTS looks particularly stunning in the late summer sunshine. *(Author)*

FKE 484C

Although it was introduced at the same time as the 275 GTB, the 275 GTS (Spyder) was an entirely different model, tracing its design ancestry rather to the earlier 250 Cabriolets and the 330 GT 2+2. Featuring the same V12 engine and technical specs as its coupé sibling, the GTS developed slightly less output at 260bhp. Unlike the GTB, which was designed by Pininfarina and the bodies hand-built by Scaglietti, the Spyder was both designed and built by Pininfarina.

Not a model to get much press, the GTS is one of those rare beauties that is a good example of practical top-down motoring combined with extremely good looks and possessing ample performance. As a result it was well liked by the rich and famous, and one can picture Raquel Welch, headscarf blowing in the wind, speeding along the French Riviera in her 275 GTS in 1964. It was just the kind of car that would attract attention, and indeed anybody would look good in a GTS.

Styling of the 275 GTS was, in fact, a mix of elements, with the front end taking its influence from the 250 Cabriolet series, while the rear end of the 330 GTC was grafted on at the back. However, far from appearing a mix of styles, this Pininfarina-designed Spyder was one of the most pleasing and balanced of all cabriolets of the period.

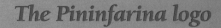 This handsome 1966 Ferrari 275 GTS was photographed outside a well-known auction house in London. *(Motor Industry Archives)*

The Pininfarina logo

Why does the Pininfarina badge still have the 'f' symbol at its centre? In the beginning the name of the company was Pinin Farina, where these two names were obviously those of its founder Battista 'Pinin' Farina, and so the 'f' letter is taken from the Farina surname.

Over the years it was decided to keep the 'f' symbol in the company's logo as this signified a continuity in the company name, linking the new Pininfarina name with its origins, while it also served to unite the two names when looking to the future.

The Pinin Farina 'f' logo has appeared on every Ferrari designed by this Turin-based studio. *(Author)*

The Ferrari 275 GTS had a wide three-seater front bench where the front passenger seat could accommodate two (rather cramped) passengers. *(Neill Bruce)*

1967 Ferrari 275 GTS/4 – NART Spider Conversion, of which only ten were built at the request of American importer Luigi Chinetti. This, too, was designed by Pininfarina and built by Scaglietti. *(Neill Bruce)*

Ferrari 330 GTC (1966)

It was not until he was 40 that Sergio Pininfarina owned a Ferrari, and this was the 330 GTC, a car that he regarded as elegant and very compact. By this stage Ferrari was making fewer and fewer 'one-offs' and was tending towards small production runs which enabled the company to concentrate on improving product quality and to better share technology between race and road models.

Introduced at the Geneva Motor Show in March 1966, the 330 model was once again a hybrid product, using the chassis from the 275 GTB, the engine from the 330 GT 2+2 (from which some design inspiration was taken), and the body a combination of the front

borrowed from the 400 Superamerica and the back from the 275 GTS. But, far from appearing a mixture of designs, the 330 GTC was, as Pininfarina put it, 'elegant and compact'.

All-round vision was excellent, thanks to large windows and a relatively high seating position when compared with, say, the 250 or 275 series. The smooth bodywork, devoid of excess flash, was simple in that it did not shout performance and aggression, but rather sophisticated touring with elegance. The car's new 4-litre V12 engine ensured progress was rapid, while air-conditioning, wood-trimmed dash, and a lavishly finished interior indicated that this model was intended for touring.

◔ **By 1969, the 365 GTC had lost its side vents. Instead the vents were located in the bonnet just below the windscreen.**

(Author)

◔ Ferrari heaven – a car park full of Ferraris! This Ferrari 330 GTC was spotted amongst thousands of Ferraris at the company's 60th anniversary celebrations at Silverstone in 2007.

(Author)

The 365 GTC and 2+2 versions (both with the bigger 4.4-litre engine) were produced towards the end of the decade, but sadly these two models had lost some of the elegance and soft styling that had graced the earlier 330 model. This is, however, fairly normal when two occasional seats are added to the rear of any sports car, such as the Jaguar E-type, which also lost some of its charm and early innocence once additional seating accommodation was added.

CAR magazine, in its report on the 365 GT 2+2, praised the car for its supreme comfort, spaciousness and sophistication, but said, 'Unfortunately, there are elements such as performance and appearance in which it is not really [good at] either.'

Designing for the Americans

If a single company could be said to have invented car design, it must be Pininfarina. This company has done more than any other to bring the industry of vehicle design into the home, but designing motor cars successfully for two markets as different as those in America and Europe is no easy task.

⋂ **Introduced at the 1966 Paris Motor Show, the 330 GTS offered a graceful top-down alternative.** *(Neill Bruce)*

⌒ **In 1970 the Ferrari 365 GT 2+2 was introduced. In its 2+2 form, the 365 GT provided a superbly comfortable and practical mode of transport for a family with two small children. Sadly, though, with its extended body the car lost some of its early charm.** *(Neill Bruce)*

Although very few could afford Ferraris, even in America, the increasingly sophisticated buyers there were nevertheless influenced by social developments such as music, fashion, and other international styling trends. Ferrari began to realise the value of the large and wealthy American economy, so (as we have seen) some models were given names that appealed directly to that market (e.g. Superamerica and California). This trend was confirmed by an unmistakable growth in road car production and an acknowledgement of American market influences in body styling.

When you look at the Superamerica and California, there is a sense that they were being designed for a different market. 'I think Pininfarina and a lot of the Italian design houses were working for American companies as well, so they had an insight into what the American market liked, and the cars tended to be a bit less functional. There is a bit more chrome than one might expect, they are a bit more showy than they were in Europe, and I think that goes all the way through to the California, even the latest California, which I think is very much an American product – it is not a European product,' revealed Dale Harrow.

He continued, 'The other thing is, if you look at the Pininfarina way of designing, it works quite well for the American market because there is a different quality of light in America, you tend to see more plain light surfaces because you get strong contrast, and I think you can see that in the way some of the surfacing was done. When I saw a second generation Corvette on the road recently, it struck me how old-fashioned it looked, even though it's a nice car, but there is something about the proportions of American stuff at that time that you can see in some of those Ferrari models. They had bigger wheels, they tended to be taller, tended to be a bit more defined by chrome, and things like that, but not overly done. There is a really nice degree of taste there – an understanding of that market but not falling into its problems, you know.'

Pininfarina was particularly good at creating very clean and defined surfaces or shapes in their designs, whereas a lot of European cars were more rounded. In America, those rounded shapes were less common as they tended to create more plain surfaces. 'I think the Pininfarina way of creating shapes was very similar [to the American way] because they were using gesso plaster, so their surfaces weren't overly sculptured,' Harrow suggested.

⌒ **The new Ferrari California has presence and striking looks, but it is more of a touring car, or one for a great day out.**
(Author)

Beauty and the beast

— PART 2

The Italians have always had a great ability to combine. They mastered the concept of 'if it looks right it is right', and I think most of the great cars have looked right whether they are Ferraris or anything else.

— NICK MASON
Ferrari owner

Ferrari in the late 1960s

In 1965 a Dino 206 P, powered by a 1986cc V6, appeared at Germany's Freiburg-Schaunisland hill climb course and won the race, beating a number of Porsche 904s, Abarths, and Lotuses. This little racer became the Dino 206 S and was designed in both open-body and closed-body forms. The 166/206 served as the basis for Pininfarina's one-off 166 Dino Speciale show car at the 1965 Paris show. Using the race car's mechanicals, the Speciale was so well received that Pininfarina continued to develop it, eventually turning it into the Dino 206 GT, the first road-going mid-engined car to come from Maranello.

The latter half of the 1960s was characterised by two models that would once again confirm the company's position as an innovative manufacturer with a knack for producing sports cars that would stun the world. One of these cars, the Dino 206 GT, was a reluctant starter and, with its mid-engine layout, represented a very courageous, if not downright risky, step into the unknown for Ferrari. The other new model, the Ferrari 365 GTB/4, or the Daytona as it would become known, was Ferrari's flagship Grand Tourer, which replaced the outgoing 275 GTB/4.

'Ferrari cars had always been connected to racing, so when the racing car's engine moved from the front to a midship position, Ferrari road cars also started moving to the same layout – two seats with a rear midship engine. This was the true Ferrari "concept" meaning,' recalled Emanuele Nicosia, a designer (from 1976 to 1985) at Centro Ricerche, a division devoted to advanced design. This facility was located alongside Pininfarina's plant until the mid-1980s when it was moved to Cambiano, about 30km (19 miles) from the Grugliasco facility.

The Dino 206 GT was almost shunned by the factory in that they did not place a Ferrari badge on the car, in order to position it well away from the company's other 'real' sports cars, conceptualising the Dino brand as a stand-alone marque. Even though the Dino name was given to the Dino 206 S race car in 1966, and it shared the same mechanicals as the later road car, the 1967 206 GT was an entirely different machine.

The Dino 206 GT represented Ferrari's first entry into the mid-engined world of road-going sports cars. It was an extremely complex accomplishment, as Dale Harrow explains: 'The Dino prototype, when you analyse it now, was a genuine step forward in terms of its design language: things like the wrapped screen with its reverse sweep, the engine package that drove the cabin space, and the general proportions of the car. And the fact that it didn't owe anything to the Grand Turismo cars that had evolved over 30 years, it really was a step change and I think if you look at that car now, it is still as beautiful as it ever was. It had beautifully controlled lines.'

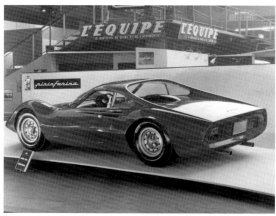

⋂ The gorgeous Dino 206 S (1966) served as the inspiration for what was to become the first mid-engined 'Ferrari' road car, the Dino 206 GT. *(Author)*

⟳ Pininfarina's 206 S prototype displayed at the 1965 Paris Motor Show. *(LAT)*

Built as a styling exercise, Pininfarina's 206 S prototype was shown at the 1965 Paris Motor Show and featured a full-width clear Plexiglas panel behind which sat two pairs of low level headlamps (perhaps showing the designer's line of thinking which would be seen on the 365 GTB/4 Daytona of 1968). Because of both styling and engineering challenges, as many as six different Dino prototypes were built between 1965 and 1967 before there was any sense of finality on the project. However, one prototype which showed the model's design close to its final shape was the 1966 Dino 206 Berlinetta GT fitted with a longitudinally-mounted V6 engine, and shown at the 48th Turin Motor Show in November 1966. For obvious reasons this model had a much longer engine cover in order to accommodate the longitudinally-mounted engine, and it was therefore built on the longer 2,340mm (92in) chassis. Its Pininfarina-designed aluminium body was hand built, being beaten on formers in the traditional manner by Scaglietti.

The twin overhead camshaft V6 engine of 1987cc, which developed 180bhp at 8,000rpm, was the brainchild of Enzo's son, Alfredo Ferrari. Alfredo, or Dino as he was known, successfully persuaded his father that the twin-cam (per bank) V6 was the way to go, and these engines went on to be used successfully in Grand Prix, Formula 2, and sports prototype machinery.

Dale Harrow again, 'We shouldn't forget fashion and trends, because this development was also reflective of what was going on on the Grand Prix circuit and was seen as leading-edge technology. So I think it is natural that there was some transfer across, particularly as Ferrari was closely associated with motor sport. It needed to have a mid-engined road car as it was running mid-engined or rear-engined race cars.'

First proposed by Sergio Pininfarina, the emergence of the mid-engined Dino moved Ferrari into uncharted territory as far as its road cars were concerned. At the time, few manufacturers, if any, made anything other than

front-engined cars with the exception of the Porsche 911 and the Lamborghini Miura (1966). Thus, with the Dino, Ferrari was able to experiment with several aspects of the car's package, such as body height, interior space, and handling.

Placing the engine midships enabled the designers to significantly lower the car's nose, giving the driver a totally different visual experience from behind the wheel. Dale Harrow expands, 'It is an interesting package, isn't it? It gives a very different experience when you drive a mid-engined car from a front-engined car in the sense that you are quite near the A-post. You don't have a long bonnet and you have got a very interesting floorpan and wheel-arches. No other vehicle manufacturers were making mid-engined road cars at that time, because I think it was technically a very difficult thing to do.'

A benefit of mid-engined and rear-engined layouts is greater flexibility in terms of aerodynamics and design,

but they do force designers to seek a compromise because these cars are generally limited to a two-seater configuration with reduced luggage capacity. On the plus side, though, the improved aerodynamics resulting from the absence of a high body sitting atop a traditional chassis (in theory allowing for a larger engine to be fitted behind the cabin) makes for greater performance potential.

In addition, relocating the engine in this way allows the designer to drop the cabin and move it forward, with the result that the driver sits lower, and as the engine height can be dropped, the centre of gravity is also significantly lower, which all points to better handling. There are also gains from better traction control, and with the exhaust system exiting directly from the engine to the rear of the car, it eliminates the need to run the pipes under the cabin along the full length of the car, reducing weight and again lowering the whole body structure.

⋂ **Thanks to the mid-engine layout, the lower height of the Dino body up front resulted in more pronounced wheel-arches which rose above the level of the luggage compartment as well as the car's waistline. This resulted in muscular haunches, which gave the car a definite sporting appeal.** *(Tom Wood)*

⌒ **From this rear three-quarter angle, the Dino's muscular lines can be seen in the well-defined front and rear wing (fender) line.** *(Tom Wood)*

The result is a lower nose, as the relocation of the engine and radiator gives the designer the flexibility to manipulate the storage space to create some luggage capacity elsewhere in the vehicle.

Dale Harrow is full of admiration for the original Dino prototype: 'In theory it is a very efficient package and, with hindsight, it must have been quite an achievement to make that work. And if you look at that stuff, it still looks incredibly fresh [today], there is not much that has dated it. I think they were doing some really striking stuff at that time. It's a revolutionary package.'

The Ferrari Dino 206 Speciale prototype was presented at the Paris Motor Show in September 1965. For Sergio Pininfarina, this model had special emotional significance, as his father, Battista, was very sick, and absent from the Turin factory most of the time. The responsibility for this project, therefore, rested entirely on his shoulders. He remembers arguing frequently with Ferrari in an attempt to get 'Il Commendatore' to accept the mid-engine sports car proposal, which offered the following advantages for the body:

- A lower bonnet and thus better visibility and lower wind resistance.
- A lower barycentre because of there being no exhaust pipes below the floorpan.
- A cabin which could be better insulated because of the absence of exhaust pipes.
- Greater internal stability from better access to the gear shift because of the new layout.

This new layout was not without its compromises, such as the noise of the engine that sat right behind the driver, and consequent reduced rear visibility. But it was through the persistence of the designers in overcoming these difficulties, and maximising the advantages of the new mechanical layout, that Pininfarina managed to create, in the Dino, a new type of production sports car for Ferrari.

The production Dino, built on the shorter chassis with a wheelbase of 2,280mm, was finally revealed at the Turin Motor Show in 1967, but would only go into production in late 1968. It featured a host of stylish details, such as slender flying buttresses (which greatly improved bodyshell strength), the reverse curved rear window, elegantly muscular lines and attractive engine cooling scoops on the flanks, which also added an element of streamlining to the sleek body. It was this latter feature, the elongated cooling ducts on the car's flanks, which were incorporated for styling as well as practical purposes, which would prevail on all mid-engined Ferraris for the next three decades.

For Sergio Pininfarina, the Dino 206 GT was a dream come true, as by his own admission he worked hard to persuade Ferrari that a mid-engined road sports car had a place in the Ferrari model line-up at that time. For Ferrari, the Dino was a landmark car, a model that separated the traditional front-engined cars produced by the company from the cars that followed. Not only was it a defining model within Ferrari, but it was also a trendsetter within that vehicle market segment. With the benefit of hindsight, the Dino was possibly the car that had the greatest influence on Ferrari's future sports car designs as the basic silhouette can still be seen in the company's current range of cars.

Alfredo 'Dino' Ferrari

Alfredo was born on 19 January 1932 and died on 30 June 1956, aged just 24. Destined to follow in his father's footsteps, and no doubt primed to take over the family business, Dino trained in engineering at the Modena and Zurich institutes, and his final thesis was on the subject of a 1.5-litre engine breathing through a three-valve per cylinder configuration. This would later form the basis of the 1.5-litre V6 Dino engine.

Suffering from muscular dystrophy, Dino's final months were characterised by bedside meetings in the hospital with Enzo and factory engineer, Vittorio Jano, in which the possibility of a Formula 2 1.5-litre DOHC V6 engine was discussed. None of the men could have envisaged the profound effect this engine would eventually have on Ferrari's sports cars well into the future.

Although Dino did not live to see his planned engine in use, his legacy would be remembered, and felt by Ferrari enthusiasts around the world.

⟃ **The 246 GT's larger engine was a welcome increase for those wanting better performance from their Dino.** *(Author)*

The significance of the Dino 206 GT

Revisiting some of our earlier observations, we can see how the Italian automotive industry was a powerhouse of design innovation. In the late 1960s and early 1970s, several design studios created some strikingly futuristic examples in automotive design, such as Bertone's Lancia Stratos 0 prototype (1970), and during this period many other aesthetically innovative vehicles were produced.

Dale Harrow shares his thoughts on this design period: 'I really admire the first Dino prototype. It was very clean, because it really was completely different. What they were doing with the mid-engined cars, they were really redefining sports cars. A lot of the front-engined cars were just an evolution of what was going on [in the market], even right back to the Cisitalia. In terms of the line and proportion, it was just an evolution, but you can see when they got to the mid-engined cars they were having to reform what a sports car was. There was a step change in the language and the possibilities in engineering, which allowed so many new opportunities in terms of aesthetics that we hadn't seen before.'

This step change came about not only as a result of mechanical and technical developments, but also because customers wanted this innovation that they had seen on the Grand Prix circuits. This groundswell of aspirations led to a complete rethinking of the car. Harrow says, 'If you look at some of the stuff that was being created at the time, it really is as fresh as the first Cisitalia, it really is something new and we hadn't seen it before. If you look at the Miura, I think it is one of the most beautiful cars. If you look at say the Dino, it no longer has anything to do with the development of a front-engined road car, it is completely different. I am just amazed at the Dino from that period, the kind of delicacies are just fantastic, it is just beautiful.'

Nick Mason agrees. 'I think Ferrari certainly sold his road cars on the back of his Formula 1 programme, so there was probably a bit of "well, we probably ought to do that". And I suspect he probably thought he would like to appear to be more advanced in the engineering of his sports cars.'

For Ferrari, the Dino created a watershed in its thinking, as this mid-engined sports car offered the market the roadholding and performance of a race car, but with the civilised attributes of a normal road-going sports car. The development of the Dino created a whole new market, not only for Ferrari but for the whole sports car industry, as the mid-engined car offered comfort, performance, and touring capabilities previously only available in larger front-engined vehicles.

⏻ The Dino 206 GT rewrote the book on sports cars in the 1960s. Except for some detailing, this early Dino GT prototype shows how little the concept differed from the final production version. This prototype has a slightly more pronounced front end with pouting lips, a longer back because of the longitudinally-mounted engine and some additional detailing around the door handles. *(CAR magazine, South Africa)*

Dale Harrow explains, 'It's very complicated. I mean, even though it is a simple design, when you look at the kind of surfacing and the way this is controlled, it is very clever, and it is so easy to get that wrong. They were doing some pretty sophisticated stuff at Pininfarina.'

Harrow is fairly critical of today's designers, many of whom have abandoned the older technology, having moved away from the artisans working with designers to create shapes and control lines very carefully, to today's reliance on 3D Alias computer programs. He continues, 'In doing so, they have lost some of that finite control where [today] surfaces are created by lines in space which are then joined up, rather than it being a kind of fluid form [process]. The other thing with computers is that you can over-detail.'

As already mentioned, the evolution of the Dino's development from the long wheelbase (2,340mm) to the final short wheelbase model (2,280mm) was not without its problems. Turning the engine from its early longitudinal position to its final transverse layout enabled the engineers to incorporate a more than useful rear trunk. The earlier prototype's engine cover would lift as one large, very cumbersome panel exposing the whole rear workings of the car, rather like a race car. But, by turning the engine sideways, it would not be necessary to open the whole back end of the car to access just the engine, and likewise one would not want to be exposed to a hot engine when retrieving personal items from the boot (rear trunk). The answer was to create two separate covers that could be lifted individually, giving easy access to the boot (trunk) or (not so easy) access to the engine bay.

The whole process of the design of the rear half of the car is the work of a genius. Behind the occupants, the reverse curved window flows into the tapering buttresses which frame the engine and boot (trunk) in a most elegant manner. An area of low pressure is created in the recess directly behind the rear window, and air flowing over the roof then draws the hot air exiting from the engine through slats in the engine cover, which is funnelled between the buttresses and over the back edge of the bodywork. The gentle slope of the engine cover from the rear window down towards the tail cleverly hides the fact that the engine had to be raised by two inches in the body because the transmission and differential, cast in a single unit, was located beneath the engine.

⋂ **The Dino's reverse curved, vertical rear window was a first on a 'Ferrari' road car. Pininfarina did a superb job of blending the various surfaces together in this complex corner of the bodywork.** *(Author)*

⊃ **A Dino 246 GT comes together on the main jig at the Scaglietti works. Ferrari dealers were treated to a tour of the Scaglietti works during their 1973 visit to the Maranello factory.**

(Neill Bruce)

The Dino 206 had few critics and was an instant hit when launched. It was thoroughly modern and struck a perfect balance between style, sportiness, and comfort. Production ran at the rate of around three cars a week from the spring of 1968, but after just 150 had been made (all of which were left-hand drive), Ferrari discontinued production the following summer. Maranello's great rival from Stuttgart produced sports cars in greater numbers, for a much cheaper price and with comparable performance, so the Dino needed to be upgraded and uprated in order to keep pace with Porsche.

More power was required, and this appeared in the form of the 246 GT, which was launched at the 1969 Geneva Motor Show, featuring a larger 2.4-litre version of the same engine. The larger 2419cc engine produced 195bhp, up from the 180bhp of the smaller 206 GT. The Dino 246 reverted to the longer wheelbase (2,340mm) of the original prototype and, for reasons of cost, the new model was fabricated from steel, which added about 50kg (110lb) to the car's weight. No doubt envisaging greater demand, the newcomer also featured a modified central chassis tube to facilitate the production of a right-hand-drive version.

Emanuele Nicosia explains the origins of the Dino 246, 'The Dino 246 came directly from the Dino Parigi, a show car presented at the Paris Motor Show. It was designed by Aldo Brovarone, the design office manager at the time I was there, and the designer of the great Cisitalia. Brovarone also made all the renderings of Fioravanti's Ferraris, such as the Daytona, BB, and 308 GTB, because Fioravanti was a mechanical engineer and not able at all to make sketches and renderings, even though he had a great sense of beauty.'

Significantly, the new 246 lost none of the elegance and style that the 206 possessed, which so often happens when a car's dimensions are summarily increased. The old adage of 'first is best' lost some of its sting in the case of the 246, because in this instance 'the second was just as good as the first' model in terms of looks, and altogether better in terms of performance.

Although Ferrari's production numbers were never high in industry terms, automobile historian Marián Šuman-Hreblay opined, 'The Italian automobile industry refused to believe that there was insufficient demand for special coachwork on mass-market cars.'

Also launched at the Geneva Motor Show, but two years later in March 1972, the Dino 246 GTS made an interesting addition to the Dino range. No doubt wanting to nibble away at some of Porsche's Targa sales, the GTS offered similar 'top off' motoring to the 911 Targa. The removable roof panel could be stowed behind the seats, but with the roof in place and no rear three-quarter windows, a bank of three stylish air vents channelled air to the rear window. The targa-roofed GTS was only available on the Series III Dino platform.

By the time the Dino was phased out in 1974, more than 3,700 of this model had been produced during its six-year production life cycle. Pininfarina readily admit that the stylistic approach of the Dino concept served as the foundation for all successive mid-engined Ferraris. Perhaps this fact serves to highlight the importance of this model.

↷ Despite using the longer wheelbase (an increase of 60mm/2¼in to 2,340mm/92in) for the Dino 246 GT, the designers were able to retain the beautifully balanced lines of the original. (Tom Wood)

↶ This shows the three different compartment lids opened – at the front is the luggage compartment while at the rear, the engine compartment lid is sandwiched between the aft luggage compartment and the cabin. Engine access on the Dino was not great. (Neill Bruce)

Changing times –
the influences of the 1960s

Indirectly, the growth of music, fashion, and the mushrooming of social expectations all contributed to the increased affluence of society in general during the 1960s, especially amongst the younger generation. Nick Mason was part of this explosion of cultural ideologies and experimentation: 'In general terms, in the '60s, pop or rock music transitioned from a working class exploitation of the teen idol movement (such as Larry Parnes' 'stable' of talent) to something weightier like The Beatles' *Sergeant Pepper* album, Cream, Hendrix, and more.'

Bob Dylan's *The Times They Are a-Changin'* (Columbia Records, 1964) confirmed for the younger generation that they were indeed living in an age when every convention could and should be challenged. This generation, the Baby Boomers, thought and believed they were different and more in tune with life than any generation that had gone before. Some were misguided, but this pent-up energy wasn't all negative, because many young creative designers were also caught up in this groundswell of new thinking.

Many middle-class students went on to be Art School educated, a developing trend during this period, and they were in turn influenced by designers, photographers, musicians, and young entrepreneurs of their day. Increasing wealth meant that Ferrari could both afford and justify the extravagant designs that appealed to the American market of this period. Though this book is clearly not just about the Ferraris of the 1960s, in many ways that decade established a platform on which several key Ferrari models were founded, making it an extremely important period in the company's journey along the road of automotive design.

The 1960s were unquestionably the decade of the supercar, and the growth in awareness of Ferrari's sports cars and the emergence of other manufacturers' products, such as the Maserati Mistral, Lamborghini 350

↻ **The Jaguar E-type Series 1 coupé offered the 1960s driver affordable sports car motoring with great looks.** *(Author)*

⊃ **Having only been introduced at the 1963 Frankfurt Motor Show, Porsche's 911 quickly won the attention of the young jet-setters. This 911 S 2.0 (1969) illustrates the exciting lifestyle of its owner.** *(Porsche-Werkfoto)*

GT and Miura, Porsche 911, and the immortal Jaguar E-type, was evidence that the market wanted this exotica. The name 'supercar' was coined during this era, which saw the sports car sector divide between ordinary sports cars and these super-fast and exclusive sports cars, which formed a very definitive genre of its own.

The task of the design houses was to provide what the buyers wanted, which resulted in the growth of a quite distinct automotive design industry that the motor manufacturers fully utilised to attract customers to their brand. This increase in demand for stylish, brutish, streamlined body styles ensured that the professional design houses of Europe were kept busy, which in turn drew on the creative young talent pool graduating from the universities and design schools. It was during this period particularly that experimentation with streamlining was prevalent, and this saw the evolution of Grand Touring fastbacks, streamlined body contouring, air inlets and outlets, NACA ducts, and tail lips, all in the name of aerodynamics and downforce.

⌒ **The Lamborghini Miura (1966–72) was the first viable road-going sports car to have its engine fitted in a mid-rear position. Its impact on the market at the time was phenomenal, as most other sports car manufacturers scrambled to copy them.** *(Automobili Lamborghini S.p.A.)*

⌒ **Designed by Pietro Frua, the Maserati Mistral Spyder (1963–70) was considered to be one of Maserati's most beautiful sports cars – the last of the company's cars to feature a six-cylinder front-engined layout.** *(Maserati)*

Ferrari steered away from establishing its own in-house design department at this time, a move which, upon analysis, probably gave Enzo Ferrari greater control over the design of his cars. Dale Harrow agrees: 'I don't think they were very keen to start their own design department, and maybe that was because they wanted to concentrate on being seen as [developing] the mechanical side, and out-sourcing the clothing.'

In this way, Enzo was the Ferrari design department as their supplier of choice, in this case Pininfarina, knew that they had to be constantly leading global trends in automotive design in order to remain the preferred supplier to Ferrari.

In the world of vehicle design, the Italian design houses such as Pininfarina, Touring, Vignale and others saw themselves as professional designers who had to observe and analyse what market trends were doing globally. They were, therefore, in a better position to interpret those trends, whereas Ferrari saw himself as a maker of performance cars and would rather leave the design element of car production to a professional outfit, which was not influenced by the internal politics within his own firm. These design studios were working as proper design houses providing a complete product design and solution service, making all manner of products such as boats and trendy household items. They were working just like a design consultancy in the broadest sense, and importantly they were working for American companies, and so they had that vital understanding of the American market, whereas Ferrari did not have that reach.

The important ingredient in this partnership recipe was that Pininfarina were able to retain their total independence while acting as a professional international design studio, but at the same time being able to work incredibly closely with the Ferrari engineers. This is borne out by the fact that Pininfarina was able to clothe Ferrari's sports cars in the most streamlined and classic shapes, while the Ferrari engineers managed to pack some of the most powerful engines of the day under the skin with all the necessary power needed to push the car along at staggering speeds.

It seems ironic that Ferrari was happy to out-source one of the most crucial aspects of the production process, that of presenting his cars in the most visually appealing manner possible. By nature, Ferrari was a controlling figure who liked to have his finger on the pulse of all aspects of production, but in this arrangement he was able to avoid any potential

➲ **A prototype Daytona design study photographed by a consulting engineer during a visit to the Pininfarina plant in the early 1960s. Tilting the body on a frame in this manner enabled the designers to observe how light fell across the body when viewed from the 'top', while still standing on the ground.**
(Motor Industry Archives)

conflicts in the emotional world of car design within his own company. He also knew that an external design house would be delivering the best possible designs one hundred per cent of the time, because they were being paid handsomely to do so.

'I suspect Mr Ferrari would come in and review things, and it would be a bit like Bill Lyons [of Jaguar] saying, "lets move this line a little bit", so there would be much more of a dialogue. But maybe this was where he was able to retain more control,' reasoned Dale Harrow.

Ferrari 365 GTB/4 Daytona (1968)

If the Dino 206 GT was considered the epitome of elegant design, embellished with exquisitely stylish detail, then it might be likened, say, to a piece of easy, but full-bodied music, sharpened with a touch of hot spicy flavouring. By contrast, then, the Ferrari 365 GTB/4 could be compared to a no-holds-barred, full-volume, untamed rock 'n' roll song by the Rolling Stones with singer Mick Jagger at his raucous and screaming best.

Dubbed the 'Daytona' by the motoring press in recognition of Ferrari's 1-2-3 finish in the 1967 Daytona

24 Hour, the 365 GTB/4, its official name, was quite different from any Ferrari produced to date. Introduced at the Paris Motor Show in October 1968, the relatively simple, almost flat-panelled Grand Tourer left behind some of that voluptuous styling so admired on the 250 series cars before it. This would be the last Ferrari thoroughbred two-seater Berlinetta to have a front engine for the next 24 years, when the 456 GT was launched in 1992. Although the 456 GT was indeed a front-engined GT, it was the 550 Maranello in 1996 that was the real successor to the Daytona, making this a gap of almost three decades.

The 1960s ushered in a culture that encouraged freer thinking, and the European car design industry led the way with new styles and concepts. Although the musicians mentioned in the analogy above would agree that music trends can be created almost overnight, car design, by contrast, requires the long-term foresight of market conditions and a substantial financial commitment by the manufacturer. In addition, new production methods and innovative technology – remember, this was the age of space exploration when technology

○ **All Daytona bodies were built at the Scaglietti works, as there was no body construction at Maranello. Here a 365 GTB/4 body shell nears completion at the Scaglietti works in 1973.**
(Neill Bruce)

threatening to crowd Ferrari off the supercar stage, and Maranello needed to respond. Sports cars with 7-litre engines were ruling the day at this point, and the 3-litre Ferraris were beginning to look a little light in the pants. Despite having potent racing machinery for the track, Ferrari had by now entered the crowded street sports car market, and they could not afford to wallow around in the middle of the pack with underpowered machinery.

Placing the Daytona in context, it was one of the cleanest and most aggressive looking Berlinettas to date, which is surprising in so far as the new model was not intended as a pure race car, and so the brutish styling may have seemed at odds with its intended market. However, there can be little argument that the Daytona ushered in a new generation of design with its angular, flatter body panels.

The starting point for the Daytona was the 330 GTC chassis. Pininfarina Chief Styling Designer, Leonardo Fioravanti, created a flowing shape to sit on top of the 330 chassis (2,400mm/94½in wheelbase) despite the fact that the 275 series was not due for replacement. His vision for this new model, which Sergio Pininfarina liked, incorporated a long tapered bonnet (similar to the 275) with a short, distinct back end that borrowed some styling from the 250 GTO and 275 models, thereby creating the classic sports car design with a long bonnet (hood)/short deck layout. Not conforming to any Ferrari norms, the breakaway design of the Daytona was once again built by Scaglietti in steel, with bonnet, boot lid, and doors in aluminium.

◯ **Daytona body shells as far as the eye can see at the Scaglietti works!**
(Neill Bruce)

◡ **With superbly balanced sporting lines, the Ferrari 365 GTB/4 Daytona was respected both on and off the track.** *(James Mann)*

and experimentation were pushing the boundaries of convention – allowed designers and manufacturers to explore previously uncharted waters.

But the new Ferrari had to be more than just beautiful, it also had to elevate the Ferrari brand to the upper echelons of the sports car tree once again, and to suppress the rising numbers of high-powered street-legal GT sports cars that could all hold their own in a straight fight with the Italian stalwart. The Lamborghini Miura and Bora, Chevrolet Camaro, Ford Shelby Cobra, Aston Martin, Jaguar E-type V12, and Maserati were all

First seen on Pininfarina's 206 GT Speciale shown at the 1965 Paris Motor Show, the Daytona featured faired-in twin front headlights arranged in pairs behind what *CAR* magazine unflatteringly referred to as a 'plastic brassiere'. This lighting arrangement was soon replaced with pop-up lights, so typical of the day. Pininfarina's design incorporated a chisel-like front end with a full-width light cluster that started on each flank with the large orange indicator lenses, and was underlined with a pair of thin bumper halves on each side. The front-end design dispensed with any traditional form of grille, which was unquestionably bold and unlike any Ferrari before it, but it served to give the Daytona an overwhelming sense of strength and power. The full-width, forward-hinging bonnet stretched back to the base of the large windscreen, which in turn was set at a very 'fast' angle.

Designed by Pininfarina master craftsmen under the watchful eye of Design Director Franco Martinengo (1952–72), the outer sheet metal was in two major pieces. The sheet metal for the front end, forward of the doors, was in one piece, being custom fitted and trimmed to each car. All sheet metal aft of the doors, including the roof, was a second piece of sheet metal. The boot (trunk), the bonnet (hood), and each door had its own skin. The large bonnet was wide and flat except for two large scoops, which allowed hot engine air to escape, but most of the hot engine air escaped from underneath the trailing edge of the bonnet, flowing up and over the windscreen.

With no side vents or scoops to disturb the smooth flanks of the Daytona, the designers created a sense of speed in the car, which looked fast even when standing

◗ **Ferrari's 365 GTB/4 Daytona had classic sports car proportions with its long bonnet and short rear dimensions.**

(James Mann)

which wasn't far off the truth. This 'thrusting' stance was confirmed with the car's short tail, which could be likened to the tensed haunches of a cat about to pounce, and a sense of movement was created by the smooth profile of the car. The strength of the Daytona was further emphasised by the chunky Campagnolo five-spoke alloy wheels, creating a look not unlike the Ferrari race cars of the period. The car's roof-line and fastback rear windscreen formed a full but undisturbed line down to the trailing edge of the boot lid. The boot offered a surprisingly practical capacity level for weekend travel, but not much else.

The 365 GTB/4 was also the first Ferrari to use fibreglass 'tub' construction to form the passenger compartment. The floor, as well as the front and rear firewalls, or bulkheads, were made of several pieces of fibreglass, cut, fitted, and bonded together and then riveted to the inner structure and sub-frame. This eliminated rust and made assembly much quicker, and was a technique that would be used on many subsequent Ferraris.

The Colombo-designed V12 engine was set well back in the chassis to provide better balance and weight distribution with its front-mid-engine position. Despite being just a two-seater it was still one of the heaviest Berlinettas to come off the Ferrari production line, claiming a mightily impressive top speed of 175mph (282kph) from its 352bhp 4390cc engine. Various motoring journals of the day credited it with a top speed

◑ Unusually slender roof pillars allowed plenty of light into the Daytona's cabin. This was quite a departure from traditional sports car lore, which normally dictated that rear pillars would be thicker and much sturdier.

(Neill Bruce)

still. A full-length swage line (at waistline height) was created which enhanced the car's sleekness and served to divide the otherwise plain flanks, but it also drew one's eyes down to that level and thereby gave the car a lower overall impression.

The roof pillars and window frames were all very narrow, creating a sense of lightness and enhancing the car's already sleek look. Its stance declared its power, with the cabin set well back in the body, and the overall impression created was that of a missile being launched,

➲ A longitudinal 'scalfatura' ran from the front wheel-arch along the flank, around the rear of the car and back around the other side, enhancing the Daytona's already sleek lines and creating a sense of continuity.

(James Mann)

that varied between 174mph (280kph) and 180mph (290kph), but most importantly the Daytona could outrun the Lamborghini Miura – just! But the Daytona had one important attribute which made it stick out in the crowd even more: it was a man's car, with a definite 'macho' image ably confirmed by the need for strong muscles when driving at slow speeds in town or when parking.

Access to the spacious cockpit is relatively easy. Firm seats ensure there is no slipping about at speed, and the driver is kept well informed of happenings under the bonnet via the vast array of dials before him. Apart from the large speedo and rev counter, six other dials were positioned in the stretched oblong binnacle in front of the driver, which might be considered a bit cluttered by today's ergonomically perfect vehicle standards, but this was true '70s style. The sporty and attractive wood-rimmed steering wheel could become treacherously

slippery in sweaty palms. The space behind the seats was intended for no more than a briefcase or for small parcels, with tie-downs for safe storage at high speeds.

In the words of Sergio Pininfarina, 'The car is very striking, the impression of movement given by its smooth profile, and increased by the longitudinal scalfatura.' The meaning of the term 'scalfatura' is a negative section swage line that runs along the side of the body, and it was a typical '70s Pininfarina design feature for Ferraris. It was used in different ways on various vehicles, but always by small section dimension.

What the Daytona did for Ferrari was to bring the company into the modern era, and, despite being of a traditional front-engined rear-wheel-drive layout, it set new standards in supercar performance and roadholding. Lamborghini had just launched its Miura (1966), a mid-engined V12 supercar capable of 172mph (277kph),

⟨⟩ **The Ferrari 365 GTB/4 Daytona was the last in a long line of traditional front-engined sports cars to come from Maranello. Ferrari was determined to end the era with something special, and they certainly hit the mark with the Daytona.**

(James Mann)

⌒ **Thirty-five years after the 365 GTB/4 Daytona ceased production, this legend shared the stage with the Ferrari 599 GTB Fiorano at the Geneva Motor Show in March 2008.** *(Author)*

but Ferrari was resisting all attempts by Pininfarina to go the mid-engined route. Enzo Ferrari had only recently agreed to the fabrication of the Dino mid-engined concept, but he did not regard this as an appropriate set-up for his 'real' Ferrari sports cars. *Road & Track* magazine said, 'The fastest – and best – GT is not necessarily the most exotic,' but they praised almost all aspects of the car as well as its blistering performance.

In the racing lightweight Daytonas, some engine tuners extracted up to 600bhp from the mighty V12. Fully nine years after the car's introduction in Paris in 1968, the 365 GTB4 Daytona was still clocking up astonishing achievements on the international stage, such as a fifth place overall in the 1977 Daytona 24 Hours with none other than Paul Newman, Milt Minter, and Elliott Forbes-Robinson behind the wheel.

A year after the debut of the coupé in Paris, the convertible model, a strikingly Day-Glo yellow 365 GTS/4 was exhibited at the Frankfurt Show. Initially the

Spyder had not been part of Fioravanti's vision, but that did not stop Scaglietti putting such a proposal before Pininfarina, for Ferrari's eventual approval.

However, the Ferrari 365 GTB/4 Daytona marked another significant Maranello milestone in that it turned out to be the last model made by Ferrari before Enzo sold his company to Fiat in June 1969. Aside from being the last in a long line of front-engined thoroughbred sports cars, the Daytona had done one other important thing: it had re-established Ferrari at the top of the supercar pyramid and as the yardstick for that sector.

When the Daytona ceased production in 1974, it made way for a new generation of V8 cars which have persisted in various forms to this day. For Enzo Ferrari, therefore, it was perhaps fitting to bring to an end a chapter in the company's history by producing one of the most striking of all the road sports cars of all time, especially as it was powered by the gorgeous V12 engine on which he had founded his organisation almost three decades earlier.

⌒ A convertible version of the Daytona was introduced as early as 1969, but not many of these cars were produced, making those original cars even more sought after today.

(John Colley)

⌒ The open-topped Ferrari 365 GTS/4 Daytona was every bit as sleek as its coupé sibling.

(James Mann)

Tail-end

A study of the rear lights from various Ferrari models in the 1960s makes for an interesting analysis and just shows how far styles moved during this decade. From small twin-stacked roundels, triples, horizontal simple to horizontal complex, this decade probably witnessed the widest variety of Ferrari lighting styles.

⏻ **Twin-stacked – 1959/60 Ferrari 250 GT SWB.**

(Author)

⏻ **Triple stacked – 1960 Ferrari 250 GTE 2+2.**

(Author)

↺ **The single round rear lights on the 275 GTB (1964) would become a hallmark of Ferrari design, this being the most used light cluster style in the company's history. It is still used today on the new 458 Italia.** *(Author)*

⊂ Triple horizontal – the 500 Superfast of 1964 had one of the most uncharacteristic of Ferrari lighting styles in the '60s. *(Author)*

↻ Twin horizontal – the Ferrari 365 GTB/4 Daytona was introduced in 1968. *(Author)*

↺ Twin horizontal (small) – first seen on the Dino 206 GT of 1967, this model is the 1970 model Dino 246 GTS. *(Author)*

⊃ Horizontal – introduced in 1969, the 365 GTC. *(Author)*

Mid engines rule

Attitude and skill are the basis of creative work, but passion is the element that gives a professional the pleasure of loving his work.

— **EMANUELE NICOSIA**
Centro Ricerche Pininfarina (1976—85)

Ferrari in the 1970s

Enzo Ferrari was dragged kicking and screaming into the 1970s, not yet prepared to abandon the traditional front-engined layout, and not fully convinced that the modern mid-engined trend would survive long enough to justify such a drastic change in thinking. While many in the press had criticised the 1968 Daytona for not having been a mid-engined model, other supercar manufacturers, including Lamborghini, Maserati, De Tomaso, Lotus, and BMW, certainly embraced the performance potential that the new engine layout offered.

It wasn't as though Ferrari had no experience in this particular field, as the 250 LM, 330 P3 and P4 race cars had shown them, in no uncertain terms, what could be achieved with a mid-engined car. However, Ferrari must have been encouraged by the market's acceptance of the Dino 206 GT (and later the 246 GT), a car that would prove itself to be a milestone model in the company's history, if ever there was one.

Since the mid-1950s, Pininfarina had enjoyed an almost uncontested period as Ferrari's designer of choice, with very few development opportunities going to other studios. Under the design directorship of Franco Martinengo at Pininfarina (1952–72), the Turin styling house was responsible for some of Ferrari's best and most iconic sports cars. However, after some considerable persuasion, and no doubt also because of his work with Fiat, of which Ferrari was now a part, Bertone was given the go-ahead to design a mid-engined sports car that more or less replaced the 206 and 246 Dino models.

Although this Dino 308 GT4 (1973) did not receive the credit it deserved at the time, as a revolutionary model it can claim to have given birth to the idea of further mid-engined Ferrari sports cars, not least the successful 308 GTB (1975) and GTS (1977), the better-known being the latter model which became dubbed the 'Magnum P.I.' because it featured in the popular US TV series of that name in the 1980s. Dale Harrow remarked, 'They must have put quite a lot of money into development at that stage, because this was the transition from front-engined to mid-engined cars.'

The general form of the mid-engined Ferrari sports cars, and for that matter most other cars featuring this mechanical layout, resulted in a lower, wider body shape because of the relocation of the engine behind the passengers, thereby lowering the cabin height.

Pininfarina, of course, translated the car's power into aerodynamically-styled body shapes which were distinctive in the 1970s and were characterised by more sharply contoured lines and a more angular look, which was in contrast to the rounded, organic look of the 1950s and 1960s.

Although work had begun on the design of a windtunnel at Pininfarina's plant as far back as 1965, it was 1970 before construction was started and it would take a further two years to complete. At the facility's inauguration in 1972, one of Sergio Pininfarina's guests of honour was none other than Bill Mitchell of General Motors, and he no doubt hoped that by showing his American visitor the modern, state-of-the-art facility he would secure some future design work from the world's biggest car manufacturer. The Pininfarina windtunnel

⌒ **Ferrari 308 GT4.** *(Author)*

⌒ **Ferrari 308 GTB.** *(Author)*

Sergio Pininfarina

Between the years 1974 and 1977 Sergio Pininfarina served as Professor of Car Body Design at Torino's Polytechnic where he had himself studied many years before. Italy's industrial north had long been a hotbed of ideas, and many students there no doubt had dreams of working at either the Ferrari or Pininfarina factories.

Although Pininfarina enjoyed what looked like a 'guaranteed' position in the market through its relationship with Ferrari, Sergio still had to sell his company's ideas to the Maranello manufacturer. Persuading Enzo Ferrari was no easy task, and Sergio's job was to convince Ferrari that his proposals perfectly matched the automaker's objectives and that the development of a particular style or model was in line with Ferrari's industrial and commercial strategy.

As a result of Pininfarina's pioneering work in the automotive sector, the Turin company understandably grew quickly, and expansion was inevitable both in Italy and elsewhere in Europe.

(the 'father' of which is considered to be Antonello Cogotti) was the first in Italy and one of the finest in the world at that time, and it proved invaluable to their work with Ferrari.

'They have always prided themselves in that sort of "form follows function", trying to make it a bit better, and so I think the aerodynamics has always been very well done there, and maybe it starts off intuitively with clean shapes,' observed Professor Harrow. The Pininfarina Aerodynamic and Aeroacoustic Research Centre, from its opening in 1972, has remained a Centre of Excellence for research and development.

Through the 1970s and 1980s, Ferrari built the 308 and 328 as its junior supercars, the 400 and 412 as a businessman's express, and the 512 BB and Testarossa as the flagship V12s. The V8 replaced the complex and more expensive V12 as the company's standard-bearer, as the eight-pot engine more easily satisfied emissions regulations in the US. According to Emanuele Nicosia, in the years leading up to and including the 1980s, the American market had some influence on concept selection, but not on design or styling – that always had to be uniquely Ferrari.

Ferrari 365 GTC/4 (1971)

Looking as though it had been designed by a committee and assembled from the parts bins of other models, the 365 GTC/4 was neither sleek nor particularly attractive. Presented at the Geneva Motor Show in 1971, the 365 GTC/4 seemed to be an effort to make it look aggressive and aesthetically pleasing at the same time – but failing on both counts in the author's opinion.

⌒ An early photograph of the GTC/4 taken by a visiting engineer to the Pininfarina colour studio. *(Motor Industry Archives)*

⌒ The 365 GTC/4's abruptly 'chopped' nose is echoed by the styling treatment of the rear end, giving it a sort of awkward, boxy appearance. *(Author)*

⌒ This side view illustrates the simple lines of the Ferrari 365 GTC/4, devoid of any air vents, embellishments or other styling elements that typically adorned some of the more classic Pininfarina cars. *(Author)*

⌒ A hint of Daytona influence can be seen in the angular rear quarterlight window and windscreen of this 1971 Ferrari 365 GTC/4.

(Neill Bruce)

➲ This 1975 Ferrari 365 GT4 2+2 was originally owned by Colonel Ronnie Hoare, Ferrari UK concessionaire.
(Neill Bruce)

Ghia – 1944 to 1973

When Giacinto Ghia died in 1944, his widow vowed to continue the company name, and she sold it to two close family friends. The company underwent several moves and changes of ownership through the 1950s and 1960s, but when financial troubles hit the company late in the 1960s, the then owner, Leonidas Ramades Trujillo, was eager to sell the business, and Alejandro de Tomaso came along just at that time.

In 1967, de Tomaso, with backing from Rowan Industries, a US corporation run by his brother-in-law, acquired control of Ghia. After the takeover there was a widespread reduction in staff, and amongst those leaving was one Filippo Sapino, who moved to Pininfarina where he was later responsible for the Ferrari 512, which was launched at the Turin Motor Show in 1971. Sapino eventually joined Ford, and when Ford bought Ghia they appointed him chief designer and then MD of Ghia, a post from which he retired in 2001.

Ghia produced some very successful bodies in the late 1960s, including the Maserati Ghibli. The Ford Motor Company purchased 84% of the company from Rowan Industries in 1970, and three years later gained full control of Ghia.

Ferrari 365 GT4 2+2 (1972), 400 GT and 400 A (1976–1985)

Introduced at the Paris Motor Show in 1972, this Grand Coupé could have been made for the American market with its large dimensions, its 2+2 configuration, and heavy disposition, which was better suited to wide open motorways than the tight Alpine passes of Europe. However, this model didn't make it to the USA at all, except for those few that were modified and fitted with the required emissions equipment by dedicated private specialist firms.

Considering the 365 GT4 2+2 was intended for sale only in Europe, it featured a most un-European body language, with its flat panels and lack of Pininfarina's typically graceful styling. Employing the three-volume or three-box style – the first box being the engine compartment, the next being the passenger compartment, and the third box being the luggage compartment – this was Ferrari's first true four-seater. It was also the most lavishly appointed Pininfarina-designed Ferrari to date. Introduced in 1972 as the 365 GT4 2+2, and going on to evolve through 400 and 400i variations, production finally ended in 1989 when the superb 412i was discontinued and not replaced.

Although the 365 GT4 2+2 was built by Pininfarina, the floor panels were fitted to the chassis frame by Scaglietti. Popular opinion has it that the chassis went straight from the local firm Vaccari, who built the chassis, to Pininfarina, but factory sources confirmed that chassis

did indeed pass through Scaglietti for the fibreglass floor panels to be fitted before being sent to Pininfarina.

While the 365 GT4 2+2 inherited its mechanicals and stretched chassis from the outgoing 365 GTC/4, the 365 GT4, 400, and 412 models were more the conceptual successors to the 1967 365 GT 2+2. The later, and almost identical looking 400 (1976) and 412 series (1985) offered larger engines, a 4.8-litre and 4.9-litre respectively, but most important, this series was now available with an automatic gearbox.

The General Motors Turbo 400 three-speed gearbox would whisk the 412 A along at more than 150mph (241kph) in absolute armchair luxury. From the introduction in 1972 of the 365 GT4 2+2 right up to the final 412 model in 1985, the exterior appearance was very similar, with the only really obvious differentiators being the small front lip of the 412, the colour-coded bumpers, and slightly higher boot-line. All models featured the very period pop-up headlamps, and all wore the Cromadora five-star alloy wheels.

Dino 308 GT4 (1973)

Luca di Montezemolo, appointed president of Ferrari in November 1991 by Fiat chairman Gianni Agnelli, conceded that the Dino 308 GT4 never really convinced him and, while he admitted that it demonstrated new thinking, he felt that it lacked the Ferrari culture. This may be a frank and rather brutal perception by Ferrari's boss, and it may even have reflected the market's sentiment at the time, but the 308 GT4 played a very significant role in the company's path down the road of mid-engined sports cars.

Unveiled at the 1973 Paris Auto Show, Bertone's wedge-shaped Dino 308 GT4 contrasted starkly with Pininfarina's curvy design heritage. The 308 represented a stunning departure from what had gone before but, unjustly, it won few admirers in its early days.

Ferrari's smaller capacity Dino 206 and 246 GTs had successfully penetrated the market for more affordable sports cars, a niche almost totally dominated by Porsche at that time. However, the Dino 308 GT4 was an altogether new type of car for Ferrari, in that not only was it aimed at the less expensive end of the market, but it also featured two additional rear seats, small as they may have been.

Importantly, though, this Dino signalled an acceptance by Enzo Ferrari that the mid-engine concept had come to stay, and that it would form part of the Ferrari model line-up for some years to come. One of the factors that helped to persuade Ferrari to move into the mid-engined market was that his competitors were doing it and he didn't want to be left out in the cold. Undoubtedly, technological and manufacturing advances made the construction of mid-engined cars for the road more feasible and cost effective at this time.

However, this was one that Pininfarina did not pen, the 308 GT4 being the product of Carrozzeria Bertone – Ferrari instead giving the two-seat 308 GTB to Pininfarina a few years later. Bertone's opportunity came following his success with the Fiat Dino 2+2, which had so impressed Ferrari. The Dino 308 GT4 was never intended as a replacement for the Dino 246; that car was the two-seater 308 GTB of 1975.

The Bertone Dino pointed Ferrari in a new direction, a departure enhanced by the 308 badge which identified Ferrari's all-new 2926cc V8 mounted behind the small rear seats. The engine's transverse layout permitted a short back end, which in turn confirmed its 'compact' description. The GT4, the first V8 used in a series production Ferrari, was also the first in a series of mid-engined V8 Ferraris that were intended to appeal directly to existing Porsche 911 customers for whom the cars from Maranello had been beyond reach.

The Bertone factor

The commercial success of the Ferrari/Pininfarina partnership was born of the long-term 'marriage' of these two organisations, which over time resulted in the creation of a special Pininfarina design language. Other design firms looking to muscle in on this relationship and grab a piece of the action would have been well advised to follow Pininfarina's typical design direction.

Emanuele Nicosia explains: 'If you look back at the 308 GT4 designed by Bertone, it was closer to the Lamborghini design language and personality than that of Ferrari. Pininfarina's design direction for Ferrari was a sinuous but powerful design trend, even during the period of Giugiaro's influential sharp-edged designs.'

Keywords in the Pininfarina design philosophy during that time were 'clean and simple', but as Nicosia admitted, 'It was not that easy to develop a clean and simple design with a strong personality.' However, Pininfarina was able to successfully create that strong Ferrari design image which gave it a precise personality, totally different from that of Lamborghini or Maserati. Even in some small but strong and important details, these design features could become precise image-referring styling icons for each model.

According to Nicosia, the Bertone-designed Lamborghini Miura, Countach, and Diablo each had a busy design language, incorporating many styling and body details that emphasised a different, but aggressive, feeling.

⟳ Rectangular rear light clusters fitted neatly under the rather geometrically straight lip of the engine cover on the Dino 308 GT4. This styling treatment differed from Pininfarina's more familiar rounded and flowing design technique. *(Author)*

◑ Bertone's styling of the Dino 308 GT4 was extremely simple and efficient, even if this did not meet everybody's expectation of what a 'Ferrari' should look like. *(John Colley)*

However, in a move to distinguish the 308 GT4 from the higher-priced Ferraris, this newcomer did not originally wear the Ferrari badge; instead it carried the Dino badge (the Dino 308 GT4 was finally badged a Ferrari in May 1976).

It is not difficult to pick out some of the design features seen on the mid-engined Lancia Stratos (designed by Bertone's Marcello Gandini), such as the high rear haunches, low front scuttle and overall wedge shape. The rear windscreen pillars have that swept-back look of the Stratos, but the 308 GT4 has the appearance of lightness, perhaps enhanced by the large windows. Bertone's 308 GT4 was characterised by its sharply creased lines, attractive air intakes incorporated in the C-pillars, that very short rear overhang, and the curt, broad, flat front end. Overall it was a crisp, clean design that was admirably executed by the Turin-based design studio. In a distant way, design cues from the 365 GT4 2+2 could also be identified in the bonnet vent and pop-up headlights.

However, Bertone's task with the 308 GT4 was not an easy one, as many other sports car manufacturers, also trying to incorporate 2+2 seating in a mid-engined concept, were to find out. It is, therefore, neither fair nor

practical to compare the GT4 to the 206 and 246 GTs, as they were entirely different models, each with their own separate market sector application.

Instead, the GT4 should be considered alongside similar compact supercars like the Lamborghini Urraco, the 3-litre V6 Maserati Merak, and the 2.4-litre six-cylinder Porsche 911.

In response to the fuel crisis, a smaller-engined Dino 208 GT4 (1975) was produced with a 2-litre V8 for the Italian market, where engine size determined how heavily a vehicle was taxed. Bertone did not change the

styling on this smaller-engined model, but because of the noticeable drop in performance the 208 did not sell well, as Ferrari drivers expected more from a Maranello-produced sports car.

The legacy, therefore, of the Dino 308 GT4 is that it established a platform on which Ferrari could base its family of mid-engined V8 sports cars that prevail in various forms to this day. The Dino itself remained in production from 1973 to 1980, by which time more than 2,800 cars had been sold, making it Ferrari's third biggest seller to date.

⌒ **A full-length longitudinal dihedral line served to give the Dino 308 GT4 some sleekness to what was a clean wedge shape.** *(John Colley)*

⌒ **Despite the Dino 308 GT4's lukewarm reception, it was in fact an important step forward for Ferrari, as this model confirmed the company's commitment to a mid-engined configuration.** *(John Colley)*

Ferrari 365 GT4 Berlinetta Boxer (1973)

In the Berlinetta Boxer (BB), Ferrari developed a fearsome car that, like good red wine, just got better with age. For more than a decade the Berlinetta Boxer road cars continued to evolve through three distinct periods, the initial 365 GT4 from 1973 to 1976, the bigger-engined 512 BB between 1976 and 1981, and the final iteration, the 512 BBi from 1981 to 1984.

First seen at the 1971 Turin Motor Show, the prototype 365 GT4 BB represented the first customer road-going sports car with this engine layout. The BB then took centre stage on the Pininfarina stand at the Paris Motor Show in 1972, and was finally ready for production in 1973.

Ferrari had built up fairly significant experience with horizontally-opposed (or boxer) race engines, as seen in the Ferrari 512 1.5-litre Formula 1 car of 1964, the 212 E sports racer of 1969, the 312 B Formula 1 car of 1970, and others. So perhaps it was inevitable when Ferrari dropped a 12-cylinder horizontally-opposed engine (or 180° V12, to be technically correct) into their latest road-going 365 GT4 BB, that it would be something special.

Ferrari had grown up on the power of the thoroughbred V12 engine, fully believing that it was the best power plant for its road and race cars. However, Porsche's mighty Championship with its horizontally-opposed engines and its latest 911 'hammer' had just been released in the form of the Carrera 2.7-litre RS road car. Once again, Ferrari felt compelled to respond, and with Filippo Sapino recently installed at Pininfarina (from Ghia), he was able to take on the responsibility for the flat-12 engined Ferrari.

The relatively low dimensions of the horizontally-opposed engine allowed the gearbox to be mounted below the engine, but this caused some headaches for the engineers as it meant that too much weight was centred above the height of the rear axle. This led to some handling problems for racing (which the 365 GT4 BB inevitably did) and, combined with the relatively high front-mounted radiator located in the nose, resulted in a weight balance front/rear of 40:60, which is why the BB was not initially successful on the track. But for road-going purposes, this problem was not noticeable.

⋃ **Ronnie Hoare (left) shows UK dealers the first production 365 GT4 BB at Carrozzeria Scaglietti, as there was no body construction at Maranello.**
(Neill Bruce)

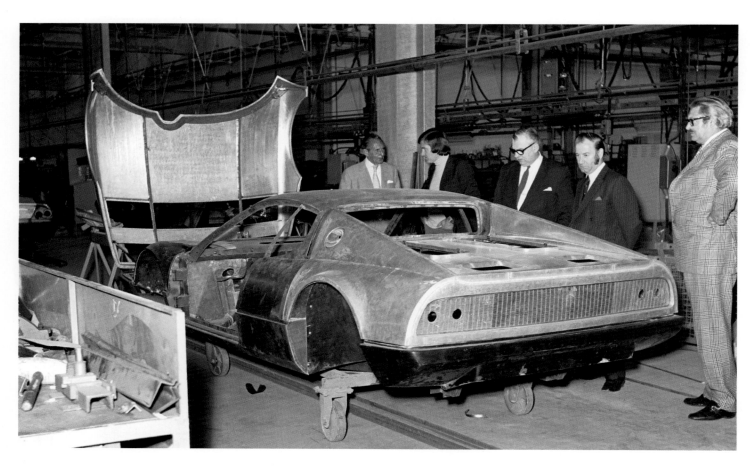

The whole body of the 365 GT4 BB is split into two overlapping shells; the upper shell is fabricated in steel, while the lower one is formed of fibreglass for functional reasons. The doors, front lid, and engine cover were fashioned from aluminium. The rear buttresses framing the vertical rear window no doubt took their inspiration from the revolutionary design of the 1965 Dino Speciale. The bodies, again designed by Pininfarina, were assembled by Scaglietti in Modena, and no matter what body colour was chosen by the customer, the lower fibreglass shell was always finished in matt black.

Sergio Pininfarina was especially proud of the fact that the company had styled such a 'history-making' car as the 365 GT4 BB, a sports car that convincingly marked Ferrari's admission into the high performance mid-engined sports car genre. With a low, flowing shape, the swage line, or groove, along its flanks enabled the eye to divide the body into two parts so that they appear superimposed, thereby creating a natural sense of speed.

Pininfarina's design represented a mixture of contemporary features and aggressive elegance, which served to highlight the strength, quality, and progress of

⊙ Ivan Bishop, Technical Director of UK Ferrari distributor, Maranello Concessionaires (on the left), examines the prototype engine of the 365 GT4 BB with three UK dealers during their tour of the factory in 1973. *(Neill Bruce)*

⊙ The 365 GT4 BB represented Ferrari's first mid-engined sports car to carry the 'Prancing Horse' logo. *(Neill Bruce)*

365 BOX

➲ **Strong rear-end styling on this 1974 model 365 GT4 BB featured a row of six lights and quad exhausts – a view most other road-users would get to see of the Ferrari supercar.** *(Neill Bruce)*

Italian automotive design in the 1970s. Like the Daytona before it, the BB sported retractable headlights, which were in vogue during the late 1960s and early 1970s, a feature also used on the Countach by Lamborghini.

Between the sweeping front wings, and linking the pop-up headlamp pods, was a brushed aluminium radiator vent, whilst the broad front lid led up to a rakish teardrop-shaped front windscreen. Flying buttresses swept rearwards from the vertical back window to the Boxer's cut-off Kamm tail, which featured a minimal

overhang and a sensational six-exhaust set-up. The triple rear light clusters found on the 1973 model were harmonious in their proportions, and were destined to become a classic style on many other sports cars. With its passionate mixture of creases and curves, Pininfarina's dramatic Berlinetta Boxer must rank as one of the most accomplished automotive designs of its era.

Because of its new engine position, the Berlinetta Boxer inevitably looked radically different from Ferrari's traditional V12 front-engined sports cars of the past. This model's importance in the Ferrari line-up, therefore, cannot be overemphasised as it paved the way for a series of Ferrari sports cars that, over the years, has consolidated the company's position at the top of the supercar pyramid. Ferrari's new Berlinetta justifiably caused a sensation when first seen in Turin in 1971, but despite some commentators lamenting the loss of the front-engined Ferrari Grand Tourer, almost all agreed that the new model was an impressive sports car.

At the 1976 Paris Motor Show, Ferrari launched a revised version of the 365 GT4 BB, called the 512 BB. Although the new model was powered by a larger 4.9-litre boxer engine, apart from a pair of NACA ducts at rocker panel level, the body was otherwise almost the same as its predecessor, causing many to mistake the 365 GT4 BB for 512 BB or the later 512 BBi (1981).

◔ **The characteristic triple rear light clusters on the 365 GT4 BB were replaced by double units on the 512 BB and BBi models.** *(Author)*

⋒ The Ferrari 512 BB was characterised by clean but aggressive lines. *(James Mann)*

⌒ The 512 BB racing version looked quite different from the road-going car with its low front air dam, wider bodywork, and large rear spoiler (wing). *(Author)*

Ferrari 308 GTB and GTS (1975)

If a single model could be credited with turning Ferrari into a mass producer of sports cars (in Maranello terms), then the 308 GTB (Gran Turismo Berlinetta) is it.

First shown at the 1975 Paris Motor Show, the 308 GTB was initially mostly fabricated from fibreglass. However, only 808 such cars were made in this way before the influential North American distributorship requested that they be manufactured in steel, as the fibreglass-bodied cars brought Ferrari's name down to the same market level as Lotus and others, although there were obvious advantages to using this modern material, such as weight-saving and rust prevention. The 308 GTB's refabrication in steel added around 100-150kg (220–330lb) in weight, but as a manufacturer of high quality, expensive sports cars, they could not afford to be perceived as middle market.

Designed once again by Pininfarina, the 308 GT is believed to be the first Ferrari tested in the company's state-of-the-art windtunnel. Chronologically, the 308 GTB followed the rather unloved, angular Bertone 308 GT4, but the GTB was in fact the spiritual successor to the Ferrari Dino 246 GT. Introduced the year after the Dino's demise, the design and styling similarities between it and the 308 GTB can be clearly seen in the silhouette of the two models. Aside from the front-end treatment, the swooping front wings (fenders), low-sweeping roofline, the streamlined lateral air intakes, concave rear windscreen, and shapely rear wings (fenders) and back end, all show remarkable similarities to the earlier Dino. After all, the two models were just a year apart, but the unmistakable signature of Leonardo Fioravanti can be seen in this iconic Pininfarina creation.

Sporting a simpler front end, the flatter luggage compartment lid and shapely fenders was a design characteristic that would survive the test of time, and can be seen still on Ferrari models today. Typical for the mid-1970s, this Pininfarina creation featured pop-up headlamps, while the 308 GTB also shared the chiselled nose of the 365 GT4 BB.

Where the Dino 206/246 had previously been the epitome of style, boasting one of the most voluptuous and seductive designs of the late 20th century, the 308 GTB was a more balanced and complete sporting package. Powered by the relatively new 2926cc quad-cam V8 (it was almost identical to the Bertone

308 GT4) mounted transversely behind the cabin but ahead of the rear axle, it was a supremely well-balanced sports car.

Taking its cue from the Dino 246 GTS, the 308 GTS (Gran Turismo Spyder/Sport) was shown at the 1977 Frankfurt Motor Show. No doubt with an eye on the commercial success of the Porsche 911 Targa, and also taking account of the roll-over safety legislation in the US, the 308 GTS was an instant success.

In 1980, a new American television series called *Magnum P.I.* was launched in which private eye Thomas Magnum (Tom Selleck) drove a 308 GTS belonging to his boss/landlord on the island of Oahu, Hawaii. Screened between 1980 and 1988, the popular series was often used as an excuse not to go out on a Saturday night, just so that one could watch the Ferrari being put through its paces. Magnum's trademark eyebrow flicker while seated behind the wheel of the red Ferrari GTS just before taking off in a shower of gravel was the mark of creative genius Donald Bellisario. Running for eight years, the 'Magnum P.I.' Ferrari had to keep pace with the latest models, and during the shooting of the first series they used a 308 GTS. The second and third series used the 308 GTSi, seasons four to six used the 308 GTSQv, and the final two series used the 308 GTSiQv.

⌒ Launched in 1977, the Ferrari 308 GTS became the international symbol for 'cool', thanks to the exploits of Thomas Magnum (Tom Selleck) in the American television series, *Magnum P.I.*
(Neill Bruce)

⌒ Pininfarina's superb Ferrari 308 GTB (1976 model). The simplicity and affordability of this model helped to bring Ferrari's high-performance sports cars within reach of a much larger potential market. The scalfatura, or concave-shaped air inlet on the car's door and rear wing (fender), became a hallmark of Pininfarina design on Ferrari's mid-engined sports cars from this time on. *(Neill Bruce)*

The 308 GTS became so well known through this popular TV series that the model was unofficially referred to as the 'Magnum P.I. Ferrari' and the success of this product placement ensured that the 308 became a household name, even for many non-motoring enthusiasts.

The 308 GTB/GTS took Ferrari into uncharted waters as far as production was concerned, as no fewer than 12,000 cars of various derivations were sold during the model's lifespan between 1975 and 1985. Selling at just below the £12,000 mark at launch, the 308 GTB was quite reasonably priced for what it was – a high quality, superbly designed mid-engined sports car that really was the sector benchmark at the time.

The practicality, wider market appeal, and affordability of the 'Magnum P.I.' model not only ensured strong sales of the 308 GTB but also served to raise the awareness of the whole brand. In fact, the commercial success of the 308 was such that it remained in production until 1985, way beyond its planned product lifecycle, when it was eventually succeeded by the 328.

In the 308 GTB/GTS model, Pininfarina created one of the most balanced and practical of all mid-engined sports cars to date, and probably since. Its compact proportions and very driveable engine made this car attractive to a much larger market than Ferrari ever planned for. The Ferrari 308 GTB/GTS eventually became the toy of choice for the playboys and playgirls of the USA, not that the Maranello firm minded.

⊃ **In 1982 the 308 was further improved with the installation of four valves per cylinder. This model was called the Ferrari 308 GTB Quattrovalvole.**

(Neill Bruce)

Prices of well-known sports cars in 1975:

Make/model	Price £
Ferrari 365 GT4 2+2	14,584
Maserati Bora	11,451
Aston Martin V8	11,349
Mercedes-Benz 450 SLC	11,271
Ferrari 308 GTB	11,112
Porsche 911 Carrera	9,996
Jaguar XJ-S	8,900
De Tomaso GTS	7,675

Source: *Autocar*

⊃ Although Ferrari's mid-engined sports cars were by now well established, it was the junior supercar, the 308 GTB of 1975, that really established the company in this market sector. *(Author)*

↻ Nicosia utilised several technical design elements on the Testarossa concept previously only seen on Formula 1 race cars, such as the collapsible side skirts (see next chapter), although these did not make it into production. *(Author)*

How do you design a Ferrari?

Emanuele Nicosia worked at Centro Ricerche Pininfarina from 1976 to 1985, where he experienced first hand how a new Ferrari was born.

At the start of a project, either a new design or a restyling exercise, the project briefing was held at Maranello with Enzo Ferrari, his staff, and Pininfarina's top management, at which the product concept was established.

Thus, Ferrari and Pininfarina were ideally placed to create a strong product development concept, thanks to their combined experience, trust and mutual respect for each other's professional expertise as a result of having worked together for so many years. This meant that the two teams could together define the car concept clearly right from the start of the product-planning phase, to be followed by multiple refining stages.

Once the car concept was completed, design briefings would be held at Pininfarina with their own designers.

Nicosia explains, 'These briefings were completely different from all the other project briefings for road cars, as design restrictions given to the designers were about strong points to be kept, and no specific direction was given for design or styling, but just the expectation of a new Ferrari that could stimulate the feelings and emotion of Ferrari lovers. The only people who could understand which proposal could satisfy that expectation were Enzo and a few of his staff from the Ferrari side, and Fioravanti and a few people from the Pininfarina side.'

Designers would then start the design research following the emotion felt at the briefings and, after a certain planned time, the first design proposal presentation was held. At that time Sergio Pininfarina and Leonardo Fioravanti (Pininfarina Design Director 1973–87) selected two or three proposals which were then refined to prepare the renderings for presentation to Enzo Ferrari in Maranello, who would then select the final design proposal.

The selected proposal would then be developed at Centro Stile Pininfarina into a full-size model, which was refined, at first, through 1/5 scale master line drawings, then through the full-size master line drawing development, which were of course all done by hand. The final modifications and refinements were done on the full-scale model before, for styling, and during the windtunnel tests, for aerodynamic analysis.

After the styling/design final approval and freezing, Pininfarina's pre-production engineering department would develop the drawings for prototype construction and for the fabrication of tools for sheet-metal hammering. Prototypes were mainly developed at Ferrari but finished at Pininfarina where all the interiors were fitted and details finalised. In the case of vehicle production at Pininfarina's production plant, the body engineering for production was developed at Pininfarina.

The red**head**

Since I was a kid, I loved those sports road cars, which, by just sticking a number on to the door, became true racing cars. This was the soul of Ferrari in my mind.

— EMANUELE NICOSIA
Centro Ricerche Pininfarina (1976—85)

Ferrari in the 1980s

For the Maranello plant this was a busy decade, during which they produced no fewer than six new road-going sports cars, three of which were really significant models for Ferrari in reaffirming their position at the top of the tree. These three included the 288 GTO, the Testarossa, and the mighty F40.

It was, though, a telling time for the industry, because many sports car manufacturers were struggling financially during the 1980s. Ferrari and Maserati became part of Fiat, Lamborghini was snapped up by GM, and Lotus had a succession of different owners, but Porsche remained relatively stable. Aston Martin, having endured its own period of troubles, was taken over by Victor Gauntlett in 1981, and after a rollercoaster ride Jaguar was taken over by Ford in 1989. However, in an unusually wise move by a large parent company during that era, the Ferrari brand maintained its independence within the Fiat Group and was allowed to get on with what it did best, and that was making the best sports cars in the world.

Despite this game of musical chairs within the motor industry, Jaguar was planning the launch of its XJ220 supercar (1989), and Lamborghini, although its Countach had been launched back in 1974, had always remained achingly more powerful than any Ferrari supercar. Besides, the Countach was designed by Bertone, and the Pininfarina studio wanted desperately to get one up on their rivals. From across the border, the Stuttgart manufacturers introduced their potent 959 in 1986, producing 450bhp, which was hailed as a technological marvel by the press and public at the time.

In effect, Ferrari was losing the performance race, and something special had to be done to regain the spotlight. Fortunately, they had the benefit of Fiat's pot of corporate money to dip into, and the result was the introduction of the three supercars mentioned above – the 288 GTO, Testarossa, and the F40 – which saw three quite different mid-engined iconic sports cars launched within just three hectic years.

But, for Ferrari, the 1980s was much more than just racing and supercars, they had ensured that their other (by now) traditional models continued to be developed to satisfy the different market segments in which they were present.

They started the decade with a new model, the Mondial 8, which fitted into their 'junior' sports car segment. Mid-decade Ferrari gave the hugely successful 308 GTB a fairly comprehensive makeover, resulting in the 328 GTB and GTS, while the end of the decade saw the introduction of the 348, a revamped and more powerful version of the 328.

The 1980s was also a period in which Ferrari consolidated its mid-engined models, as there was no appetite for the development of a front-engined Grand Tourer during this time. Nicosia sheds some light on this: 'The front engine cars were not considered at all: the only front engine car designed during that time was the Pinin show car which was Pininfarina's concept proposal. Ferrari very much appreciated the Pinin concept, but didn't feel it could invest a huge amount of money to produce something that was not a real Ferrari.'

Those were some mighty strong words coming from a company that had established itself on the front-engined rear-wheel-drive format race car. The solution within the Fiat Group was to put the 2927cc V8 Ferrari engine into the Lancia, which resulted in the Thema 8.32, but as Nicosia comments, 'The alternative that I never understood and agreed with was the Lancia Thema Ferrari.' The boys at Lancia were no doubt very happy.

Upon reflection, while other sports car manufacturers struggled through the 1980s, Ferrari, by contrast, busied itself with a growing range of models that satisfied an impressive variety of market segments with quality products.

Mondial 8 (1980)

Making its appearance at the 1980 Geneva Motor Show, the Mondial 8 shared more of its styling, layout, and market positioning with the 1973 Bertone-designed 308 GT4. Although it was powered by the same engine as the 308 GT4 (and 308 GTB), the Mondial featured a 2,650mm wheelbase, whereas the older car was based on a shorter 2,550mm wheelbase.

Also developed with the North American market in mind, with its 2+2 configuration, the Mondial 8 was given the same lukewarm reception, by both press and public, as the 308 GT4 received. With its slightly higher roofline, the Mondial offered excellent all-round visibility, but at the cost of a slightly less flowing design.

The Mondial, designed by Pininfarina, was not regarded by Luca di Montezemolo as one of Ferrari's best, as he saw it as a reinterpretation of the 308 GT4 which did not take the brand forward sufficiently. Some

↷ Ferrari's Mondial 8 was initially given a lukewarm reception when introduced at the Geneva Motor Show in 1980, mainly because of its somewhat timid and unassertive styling.
(Neill Bruce)

↶ Mondial engine changes paralleled the 308 GTB, and in 1982 the Mondial received the Quattrovalvole (QV) upgraded engine.
(Neill Bruce)

⊃ The Mondial 8 was the first road-going Ferrari to receive the 'slatted' air intake styling treatment, a feature that would be picked up on the Testarossa and others in the future. *(Author)*

felt that something didn't ring true with the model, as Emanuele Nicosia points out: 'The Mondial 8 was almost a commercial failure because Ferrari's customers couldn't accept a different solution for a true rear/mid-engined Ferrari, other than one with two seats.'

A hallmark feature of the model was the horizontal slatted air intakes on each behind the doors, which served to unite the central part of the body with the rear section through the streamlined intake styling. A strong similarity with the 308 GT4 could be seen in the front-end treatment, in the flat luggage compartment lid and pop-up lamps, also featuring a full-width slatted styling feature which ran between the wheel-arches.

From a straight-on rear view, the Mondial was perhaps closer to the 308 GTB, with its convex rear windscreen and round lamp clusters. Although the overall design was clean and crisp, it lacked the aggressive sporting stance of the 308 GTB, but then it was a 2+2 vehicle, and sports cars are always a compromise in some aspects.

⊂ In using the 'Mondial' name, Ferrari was leveraging its sporting heritage from the 1950s, but being a 2+2 the Mondial 8 had no sporting pretensions. Launched at the same time as the Berlinetta, the Cabriolet should by rights have been a popular and fun proposition, but it failed to sparkle. This Cabriolet is a 1984 model.

(Neill Bruce)

Ferrari 288 GTO (1984)

The year 1984 saw the re-emergence of a pair of iconic Ferrari names, with 'GTO' and 'Testarossa' being applied to two of the manufacturer's fastest road cars to date. These true-blooded sports cars were the creative work of Emanuele Nicosia, who was a designer at Pininfarina's advanced design studios between 1976 and 1985. 'Those two projects stemmed from my dual aspirations to create an innovative substitute for the

BB, and to revive the tradition of the road/racing GTO,' explained Nicosia.

One's first impression is to label the 288 GTO as a reworked 308 GTB, which in one sense it is, but the similarities are in fact quite limited. For starters, the wheelbase is 2,450mm (the 308 was 2,340mm), necessitated by installing the engine in a longitudinal rather than a transverse position as in the earlier car. Another surprise was the engine capacity, which at

↻ This is the final rendering by Emanuele Nicosia to finalise the sketches of this model. The GTO was developed at Maranello by Mauro Forghieri, and by the sheet-metal 'artists', under the direction of Leonardo Fioravanti, working on the Nicosia sketches (just sketches!). In the meantime, with the prototype under development, Nicosia felt the need to finalise the sketch work shown here.

(Emanuele Nicosia)

➲ Front and rear views of the 288 GTO show its 308 GTB heritage. *(James Mann)*

2855cc was more than a full litre smaller than the 308 of 1975. The awesome 400bhp power was, however, delivered courtesy of two turbochargers, giving this iconic sports car a top speed of around 190mph, or just over 300kph.

'One Ferrari that had a strong personality was the 250 GTO, so my proposal for the 288 was to continue that image, even though the new GTO was starting from the 308 concept. That excited Enzo Ferrari so much that he decided himself to proceed with the proposal,' Emanuele Nicosia recalled.

Ferrari announced the arrival of the 288 GTO at the 1984 Geneva Motor Show before a heaving mass of journalists. Initially designed as a Group B racer, hence the 'O' (for omologazione), the 288 didn't actually see competition in the manner intended by the factory, because the premature end of the Group B race series meant that the GTO never raced. Instead it was sold as a road car with phenomenal performance. Homologation required that 200 examples be built, but in the end a total of 274 cars were produced.

'The 288 GTO body was completely developed in the racing department at Ferrari due to the strong mechanical importance that this model should be like a true Ferrari racing car,' said Nicosia.

Constructed from a welded tube chassis and Kevlar body, the 288 was immediately lighter than its steel-bodied 308 sibling, whose general design it shared. As this car had been intended as a Group B racer, the fact that it ended up being sold as a road-legal car made it Ferrari's first turbocharged road-going supercar. Ferrari felt that it was important to keep the styling of the 288 GTO fully recognisable and close to its mid-market bestseller, the 308 GTB, thereby maintaining the car's links with its Gran Turismo character.

According to Nicosia, evidence of the car's intended deployment in competition is the fact that the 288 featured a Formula 1 concept that saw the rear suspension fixed to the engine as well as the rear wall of the 'greenhouse'.

Maintaining a close likeness with the 308 had its problems for the design team, as the car was both wider

⋃ **The Ferrari 288 GTO carries its increased size well, disguising the quite different running gear with its superb styling.**

(James Mann)

and longer than the design on which it was based. The body width of the GTO was 1,910mm/75in (the 308 was 1,720mm/68in) and length was 4,290mm/169in (4,230mm/167in), but height was the same at 1,120mm/44in. As well as this, its wheelbase was 110mm/4¼in longer because the engine sat in a north/south position, and crucially, with the rear overhang made shorter to compensate for this, the requirement of proportionality became more difficult to achieve. To complicate things still further, the GTO uses the 308's front windscreen and doors, which serves to highlight the similarity between the two cars, but equally it underlines the difficulty in using common body panels in a proportionately larger body. This must have given Leonardo Fioravanti and his team at Pininfarina no end of headaches, but the end result is all the more commendable as the proportions in the GTO are every bit as beautiful and flowing as the more compact 308 on which it is based.

Both models featured similarly streamlined engine air intakes along their flanks, but the 288 was fitted with a deeper front spoiler and a more pronounced rear spoiler to improve downforce.

In his book *Ferrari Supercars*, Nathan Beehl says, 'Fioravanti claims that the biggest problem was the proportional changes created by the stretched areas between the door and rear wheel-arch.'

The assertive, sporting looks of the 288 GTO were enhanced by the diagonal air vents on the lower rear wings (fenders) to allow hot engine air to escape, while the wings themselves were wider to accommodate the bigger rubber (front 255/55 VR16; rear 265/50 VR16). Also immediately noticeable were the 'flag' mirrors necessary for improved rearward vision owing to the lower seating position. The GTO's aerodynamics were honed in Pininfarina's own windtunnel and, although Ferrari will not reveal this figure, it was sufficient to make this car a strong contender in the Group B class. The car's effectiveness was further enhanced by a smooth undertray and a deep chin spoiler, while engine cooling was further improved by the multi-slatted engine cover which hinged at the rear. The rear end was finished with a pronounced tail lip, and in this respect bore a stronger resemblance to the 250 GTO of 1962.

The 288 GTO represented a major step forward in the field of advanced body structure, as the panels

consisted of advanced composite material comprising Kevlar and Nomex. Both DuPont products, these two materials, used in the manufacture of bullet-proof vests and fire protection products, are also used in the construction of Formula 1 bodies because of their high strength-to-weight ratio. For Ferrari, then, the 288 GTO represented, almost unintentionally, a huge step forward in the development of their latest road-going family of supercars.

Being introduced more than 20 years after the original 250 GTO, some asked whether the name 'GTO' was justified and if the 288 could be compared to the 250 of 1962. The use of 'GTO' cannot really be disputed as the 288 GTO was originally planned for competition use until the rules changed, so the homologation link was a valid one. What could be argued, though, was that the 288 never did rack up the race victories that the 250 GTO did, and the earlier car was a front-engined racer while the 288 had a mid-engine set-up. These two factors amount to differences rather than similarities, and one can draw one's own conclusions, but there can be little doubt that the 288 GTO was a very significant supercar in the Ferrari line-up, and it came into existence at an important time for the company.

The Ferrari 288 GTO had a much shorter rear body overhang than the 308 that inspired it. This car is the 1984 British Motor Show car.

(Neill Bruce)

⊃ The beauty of the Ferrari 288 GTO belies its awesome performance potential. This is the ex-Eddie Irvine car (chassis 55729). *(Neill Bruce)*

⊍ So much of the 288 GTO was quite different from the 308 GTB. Under that rearward-opening engine cover (the 308 opened forward) sat a twin turbocharged 2.8-litre V8 engine. *(James Mann)*

On the naming of the 288, Nick Mason had this to say: 'We all know exactly which car we are talking about when we say "GTO". I thought it was a real shame that they then made a new GTO, because the 288 GTO is actually rather a nice car, but it almost suffers from being not quite as important as the original.'

Just as the original Dino, which Ferrari was at first uncertain how to package and market, went on to inspire a whole family of mid-engined cars, which became the backbone of the Ferrari family, so too the 288 GTO, which originally could not be used for the purpose intended, went on to form the conceptual platform for a raft of new supercars, including the legendary F40, F50, and Enzo models. South Africa's influential *CAR* magazine called it 'a contribution to history' – enough said.

Ferrari Testarossa (1984)

To appreciate the impact that the Testarossa had on Ferrari's future when it was introduced at the Paris Motor Show in 1984, one must first understand the state of the supercar market in the mid-1980s.

The automobile industry had gone through the oil crisis of 1973, which had resulted in an avalanche of smaller, more economical cars coming on to the general market. This had seriously dented sales in the sports car world at the time, as manufacturers groomed people to focus more on fuel consumption and sensibility, rather than impressive performance figures.

Nevertheless, in contrast to this, the sports car market enjoyed a boom in the 1980s. There was the Aston Martin V8 Vantage, Porsche 959 and 911 Turbo Coupé 'slant nose', Jaguar XJR-S, Lamborghini Countach, DeLorean, and many others which came on the scene during that time. If not all in the supercar bracket, this short list is indicative of the scale of activity in the sports car market, and Ferrari needed to stay ahead of the game.

The Testarossa (one word) was, in fact, Ferrari's answer to most of the sports cars mentioned above, and what's more, it had shiploads of heritage to draw from. The name 'Testa Rossa' (two words), which is Italian for 'Red Head', harks back to the 250 Testa Rossa of 1957, a 3-litre V12 race car which ranks

as one of Ferrari's most successful competition cars ever. Once again, as Ferrari had done with its 'GTO', it recreated the magic of past glory by naming its new flagship road-going supercar after the legendary 1957 race car.

The Testarossa's designer, Emanuele Nicosia, explains the thinking behind his design for this car: 'My Ferrari design concept is directly connected with racing and Formula 1 cars: I have always transferred some Formula 1 features to my Ferrari road car proposals and, at the time of the Testarossa project, this Formula

⟨⟩ **The Testarossa's extremely low profile ensured an excellent aerodynamic package.** *(James Mann)*

⟨⟩ **Ferrari's Testarossa raised the bar in the supercar performance stakes.** *(Author)*

1 concept was strongly connected to ground-effect solutions. This stimulated the need to work out a design feature concept that shouldn't just be in the car's appearance and styling, but it should also be useful and real. This resulted in the side wing profile surfaces! In the original side view sketch, the car adopted a sort of retractable mini-skirt which could come down automatically when the car exceeded a certain speed (like the Porsche 911 rear spoiler).'

The new Testarossa, however, was not intended for competition, as Ferrari's road cars in the 1980s were not manufactured as cross-over road/race cars. A more sophisticated profile of customer had emerged in the previous decade, one who wanted to be seen in a Ferrari but had no intention of ever testing its performance

capabilities. A growth in personal wealth had enabled an increasing number of potential customers to consider a Ferrari, or any other supercar for that matter. In the 1980s, a Ferrari customer was more likely to be wearing a pinstripe suit or high heels and a mini-skirt, than a pair of racing overalls. Ferrari knew this and embraced this new band of potential customers by making even their supercars easier to drive, with more comfortable and luxurious interiors, and the Testarossa was no exception.

The Testarossa represented several departures and advances in both design and mechanical details. The new model was powered by an uprated version of the 512 BBi's 180° V12 (1984) of 4,943cc which was also mounted longitudinally. But far from being just a revamped version of the earlier model, the Testarossa had its radiators moved from the front to a lateral location on either side, just ahead of the rear wheels. The benefit of this move was twofold. It eliminated the need for any plumbing, which carried hot water under the cabin in one direction and cooler water in the other. It also enabled the designers to improve the car's luggage-carrying capacity up front, necessary for those all-important weekend getaways.

The Testarossa's cabin remained within the proportions of the 512 BBi, and the added width of the car below the waistline created quite substantial and relatively high rear haunches. Pininfarina sculpted this into an elegant feature, which started from immediately behind the front wheels and ran right through to the back of the car. As a result of the high rear bodywork, a single, electrically operated rear-view mirror mounted on twin fingers was located half way up the front window frame, as a wing-mounted mirror would have been too low to give the driver a sufficiently good view to the rear.

The relocation of the radiators gave Pininfarina the opportunity to create an unusually bold air intake feature, which stretched almost the full length of the car's flanks between the wheels. Five longitudinal slats added to the streamlining effect thus created, and Pininfarina also claimed that this added to the Testarossa's aerodynamic efficiency. Viewed from above, the Testarossa had an almost wedge-like shape as the rear track, at 1,660mm/65¼in, was significantly wider than the front track, which measured 1,518mm/59¾in. Therefore, the gentle outward progression of the car's flanks towards the rear not only allowed for larger and more

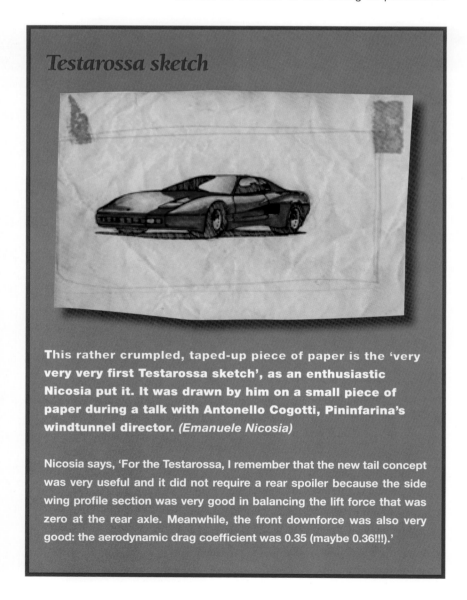

Testarossa sketch

This rather crumpled, taped-up piece of paper is the 'very very very first Testarossa sketch', as an enthusiastic Nicosia put it. It was drawn by him on a small piece of paper during a talk with Antonello Cogotti, Pininfarina's windtunnel director. *(Emanuele Nicosia)*

Nicosia says, 'For the Testarossa, I remember that the new tail concept was very useful and it did not require a rear spoiler because the side wing profile section was very good in balancing the lift force that was zero at the rear axle. Meanwhile, the front downforce was also very good: the aerodynamic drag coefficient was 0.35 (maybe 0.36!!!).'

⊃ **Borrowing its 'Testarossa' name from the 1950s racer was justified, as this car boasted a top speed of just under 186mph (300kph). During the course of production (around 1986) Ferrari switched to two wing mirrors midway up the A-pillar, as seen with this 1991 model.** *(Author)*

⋃ **The Ferrari Testarossa's ultra-wide rear stance was because of the flat engine layout, or 180° V12 to be correct. When the car was first introduced in 1984 it had a single high wing mirror on the driver's side, and these models became known as the 'flying mirror' Testarossas.** *(James Mann)*

Emanuele Nicosia recalls some early Testarossa stories

The creation and ultimate styling of the Testarossa supercar was significantly influenced by two enthusiastic designers who would meet on Saturdays at Pininfarina's Centro Ricerche offices. It was during these emotionally-charged and informal meetings that the ideas, styling, and form of the car was discussed and thrashed out.

Nicosia recalls, 'For example, the first time I thought about this car's relationship with Formula 1 was on a Saturday, when I used to go to the design studio. On Saturdays there were no other people there and you could get deeper into the project as the feeling and mood was different from normal weekdays with the usual noise during working hours. Somebody else who used to come over on Saturdays was Leonardo Fioravanti, the Centro Ricerche managing director and my direct head.

'We used to talk about cars, racing and our experiences because, before being the company manager, he was a car enthusiast like me. Both of us used to race years before and he told me about his races in a Fiat 1110, and I would tell him about my races in a Fiat Giannini 690 Group 5 "long tail". You cannot imagine the feeling and emotion that was flying around! As a result, we agreed that the new street BB (still not named Testarossa) should be like a top racing car, a Formula 1. That's why one side view among the sketches of the first design phase had the retractable mini-skirts like the actual ground-effect Formula 1 of that time.'

Originally, the side radiator air intakes did not have the horizontal bars – these were added because of US safety regulations relating to the possibility of 'hooking' pedestrians, and they became a characteristic design feature. They were also adopted for use on the tailgate. 'At that point it was decided to hide the rear lamps under those bars which were painted black to emphasise the hot air outlet area: the typical round rear lamps could not match the horizontal lines in a suitable way, so it was thought that it was better to hide them to underline this Ferrari's unusual and advanced styling concept,' Nicosia pointed out.

He also explained how the new design features were intended not just as 'stylish surfaces', but also as practical aerodynamic features. The horizontal bars on the side air intakes also had the precise aerodynamic task of cleaning the side flow from whirl air to increase the quantity, and quality, of the air collected and diverted to the oil-cooling and water-cooling radiators.

In the same way, the unusual position of the original side rear-view mirror, about halfway up the window-frame, was for two main reasons: to avoid increasing the already busy airflow in the area where the top and side airflows meet, and to have a clear rear view over the wide rear wings (fenders).

⮑ A Testarossa attending Ferrari's 60th anniversary celebrations at Silverstone in June 2007. *(Author)*

effective air-intake cavities which fed the radiators but also accommodated the wider axle requirements of the boxer engine. Larger rear wheels were also necessary to better handle the car's increased power and consequent roadholding capabilities. By shifting the engine-cooling radiators from a front to a mid-position, this brought a reduction of the moment of polar inertia, which was noticeable in a supercar of this potential.

Undoubtedly, the Testarossa marked a clear change of direction in Ferrari design, brought about by the search for solutions to technical problems which in the end led to innovative and distinctive design features. The relocation of the radiators enabled the designers to 're-use' the front grille for other purposes, as Ferrari wanted to retain the link with their Gran Turismo heritage. This frontal feature, therefore, incorporated air-collection ducts for brake cooling and air-conditioning, while the grille housed the front indicator and parking lights. The rear end of the Testarossa also came in for some radical un-Ferrari-like treatment, featuring full-width slats, which incorporated the rear light clusters. This feature rather complemented the lateral air intake slats, creating a more or less continuous theme around the car.

Sergio Pininfarina praised this successful blending of technology and style in the ultra-modern Testarossa, claiming that this interactive process resulted in the creation of the unique shape that this iconic and elegant Gran Turismo model has come to represent.

Ferrari's 1984 Testarossa was a true supercar in a long line of superb high-performance sports cars to come from the Maranello factory. This example is the British Motor Show car from that year. *(Neill Bruce)*

Ferrari 328 (1985)

Introduced at the 1985 Frankfurt Motor Show, the 328
was really a refreshed 308. Available in both GTB and
GTS guises from the outset, the 328 featured some
revised styling changes, such as the grille and front
bumper, which was now colour-coded to the body.

Perhaps the 328 was not sufficiently different from its
predecessor to really be called a new model, but it did
boast a larger 3.2-litre V8 engine mounted transversely,
just as in the 308. The overall styling was more rounded,
and the new model was credited with a better ride and
improved performance and handling, thanks to a host of
upgrades under the skin.

As a tribute to the brilliance of the initial design, the
308/328 was on sale from 1975 through to 1989, during
which time a total of almost 20,000 cars from both
model variants were produced.

Ferrari F40 (1987)

It had been 40 years since the founding of the company, and for a manufacturer like Ferrari it was too good an opportunity to miss. Something special would have to be produced, and by golly it was. The F40 was a no-frills, street-legal supercar that might have put some race cars to shame, given the opportunity.

Aged 90, and knowing that he did not have long to live, Enzo Ferrari summoned his design team and gave them the brief to create the 'ultimate Ferrari'. Styled under the watchful eye of Pininfarina's Leonardo Fioravanti and honed in a windtunnel, the F40 was a development of the 288 GTO Evoluzione.

Destined to occupy the front row of the forthcoming Group B grids, the 288 GTO Evoluzione was seen as a potent race car which would have competed against the likes of Porsche's 959. In turn, the Group B class was intended as the platform for showcasing the company's technology, and it was a great disappointment to racing fans that this contest did not materialise, as the motor sport authorities canned the Group before a wheel had been turned in anger.

To place the F40's development in context, the mid-1980s was a turbulent time in the automotive world, with the sports car market being one of the most risky areas of the market. In 1986, General Motors bought Lotus, while Ford acquired 75% of Aston Martin the following year. A year later Ford purchased outright the Jaguar company, which serves to highlight the precarious nature of the upper end of the market at the time. It could be argued, however, that manufacturers such as Porsche and Ferrari were not quite as vulnerable as the rest of the market, since their niche products were aimed at a very small sector of the specialised sports car market.

⌒ **Ferrari's 288 GTO Evoluzione photographed at Silverstone. This model gave birth to the F40 concept.** *(Author)*

⟲ **Unpainted body panels are fitted to a painted F40 chassis, with a more complete F40 visible in the background.** *(Neill Bruce)*

⟳ **An F40's body and frame awaiting final assembly at the Ferrari factory, with body panels on the right ready for fitment.** *(Neill Bruce)*

'The F40 was the design of [Pietro] Camardella, who was one of my design staff in 1986 at Design System, and actually he is now design manager at CRF (Centro Ricerche Fiat),' explained Emanuele Nicosia.

Designed with aerodynamics in mind rather than excessive power, the F40 was the ultimate in smooth shapes (at least in Ferrari's world), and it was very much a creation of its time. The late 1980s saw great advances in Formula 1 technology and lightweight materials, and Ferrari was determined to bring these benefits to the F40.

The car's frontal area was reduced, and the super-smooth luggage compartment lid, being convex in shape towards the outside, easily diverted air over the clean

surface and towards the rear wing element for maximum downforce. Two large NACA ducts punctuated the otherwise smooth boot lid, while a deep front spoiler enhanced front-end aerodynamics. A shallow centre grille with side ducts for brake cooling featured in this simple but efficient front end, while the indicator and parking lights sat behind fixed clear lenses in the wings (fenders) immediately below the customary pop-up headlamps.

One can see the 288 GTO heritage in the F40 from the front three-quarter and side views, but Pininfarina did a superb job of modernising this supercar and preparing it for the 1990s. Airflow drove the styling, and this can be seen in the extremely 'fast' windscreen angle and, with a roof height of just 1,125mm (44in), the F40 was just 5mm (0.2in) higher than the 288 GTO. The ultra-wide frontal section gave way to large exit vents for the front

brakes just ahead of the recessed A-pillars. The flanks of the F40 featured two prominent NACA ducts, the large upper duct serving as the air inlet for the engine, while the lower one fed air to the rear brakes.

The large engine cover was made of Plexiglas so that the engine in all its glory was fully visible. A substantial amount of heat was generated by the twin turbochargers, and the engine cover was extensively slatted to aid cooling, while the rear of the engine cover, where the light clusters were mounted, was fabricated from a lightweight mesh to further aid the escape of hot air from the engine compartment. Access to the all-important mechanicals was excellent, as the whole back end, hinged at the roof, lifted as a single unit to enable repair or maintenance work to be carried out.

The F40 was formed entirely by its function, reflecting some of the key conceptual values of the 288 GTO from

⌒ Although the Ferrari F40 followed in the footsteps of the 288 GTO and the Testarossa, it borrowed very little from its predecessors in terms of design, and its own radical design immediately dated the GTO and Testarossa, lifting Ferrari into a league of its own. *(James Mann)*

⌒ Ferrari F40 pop-up headlamps. *(Author)*

F40s gather – 44 of these extremely sought-after sports cars attended Ferrari's 60th anniversary at Silverstone in June 2007. *(Author)*

The Ferrari F40's twin turbocharged 2.9-litre engine differed in both bore and stroke from the 288 GTO, and in terms of performance it would almost have overtaken the Testarossa in full flight with a gear to spare, reaching a top speed of 201mph (324kph). *(James Mann)*

which it descended. For instance, its near-race status and the extensive use of state-of-the-art technology served to propel this supercar into a new performance sphere. Everything about the F40 meant business, and the focus was on unifying driver and machine to deliver the best possible driving experience.

High-speed stability rather than terminal velocity was a primary concern, and this is confirmed by the designer's attempts to smooth the airflow over the body and to direct air to the prominent high rear wing. It has been said that the F40 is rather like an open-wheel road-going race car with a body, which is probably a fairly accurate description for the car. It had a partial undertray to smooth airflow beneath the radiator, front section, and the cabin, while a second undertray with diffusers was located behind the motor to encourage underbody air to escape quickly. The engine bay was not sealed because of the high heat levels there. These factors combined to give the F40 a drag coefficient of 0.34, an impressively low figure for such a car, with lift being controlled by its front and rear spoilers.

Although this book is not about the technical specifications of each Ferrari (these are well covered in many other publications and magazines), some mention of the awesome power of the F40 is justified. The car's 2936cc V8 twin-turbocharged (sequentially) engine sat in a longitudinal position just behind the cabin and produced 478bhp, which could power the F40 from

⊃ Apart from its awesome engine power, the F40's performance also owed a lot to its superb aerodynamics. The rear spoiler (wing) was non-adjustable, the Ferrari engineers thinking that owners might be tempted to adjust the spoiler angle themselves and upset the downforce crucial to the car's stability at speed. *(Author)*

⋂ Discreet NACA ducts in the luggage compartment lid of the Ferrari F40 fed air to the cabin. *(Author)*

⋃ Airflow along the flanks influenced the design of intake vents and exterior mirrors to ensure adequate cooling for the engine and turbochargers, while still allowing sufficient air to pass over the large rear wing. *(Author)*

standstill to 125mph (200kph) in 12.5 seconds, while the 0-100kph (62mph) dash took just 4.1 seconds.

Like its predecessor, the 288 GTO, the F40 held the record for the fastest production road car in the world (1987–9) with a top speed of 201mph (324kph), and was the first road-legal production car to break the 200mph (322kph) barrier.

If one required proof that beauty and function can co-exist in one car, the F40 is perhaps one of the better examples. As a celebration of the company's 40th anniversary, the F40 was available only in 'rosso corsa' (race red). It was the last car to be commissioned by Enzo before his death, and symbolically, as in former times when a father might call his sons to his bedside when he realised the end was nigh, Ferrari summoned his trusted dealers to Maranello for a closed viewing of the supercar in July 1987. No press were allowed to attend this viewing, and those staff and dealers who were there were faced with having to keep the lid on the details of this dramatic new supercar until it could be publicly revealed at the Frankfurt Motor Show in September of that year.

Enzo Anselmo 'Il Commendatore' Ferrari
20 February 1898 – 14 August 1988

Enzo Ferrari had a desire to race cars from a very young age. In fact, it would be fair to say that he 'lived to race', but not necessarily with himself behind the wheel.

Born in Modena, Ferrari grew up with little formal education, but as with many young men of the time he was called up to fight in the Great War of 1914–18. Illness prevented him from serving in the forces for long, though, and he returned home to seek work. He started with Alfa Romeo in 1920 and raced in local competitions, where he showed some flair.

However, upon realising that his future lay not in the driver's seat but in team management, he shifted his focus to running the Alfa team. In 1937, Alfa took the management of the factory team back from Ferrari, which forced him to work under the Director of Engineering. Unhappy with this set-up, Ferrari soon left Alfa, but a clause in his termination contract prevented him from working under his own name for four years. In 1940 he set up the company Auto Avio Costruzioni and proceeded to build the 815 race car for that year's Mille Miglia.

The Second World War intervened, during which time Ferrari turned his attentions to manufacturing industrial machinery, but with the end of the war Ferrari set off at a great pace as if to make up for lost time. The rest of the Ferrari story insofar as it concerns the manufacture of racing and sports cars is contained within the pages of this book, so there is little value in summarising those activities here.

Slowly but surely, Ferrari gained the respect of the racing industry, a point that he was very keen to drive home to his critics and disgruntled previous employer, Alfa. Ferrari's importance in the sports car world has been seismic, and

Enzo Anselmo Ferrari. *(LAT)*

he continually set performance and sporting benchmarks that the rest of the industry could only aspire to.

In his role as father, Enzo's life was dealt a cruel blow with the loss of his son 'Dino' on 30 June 1956, an event that affected him for the rest of his life. However, Ferrari continued to produce breathtakingly beautiful sports and racing cars through the decades, establishing a loyal band of dedicated enthusiasts of the brand that few manufacturers could match.

Ferrari died on 14 August 1988, leaving many people wondering whether the motoring world would ever see another entrepreneur quite like 'Il Commendatore'.

↻⤷ A grand total of 44 F40s were present at Silverstone on the occasion of Ferrari's 60th anniversary celebrations in June 2007, with 42 attending the FOCGB 40th anniversary parade – a world record! *(Author)*

Ferrari 348 (1989)

The 348 TB and TS will go down in history as the first model produced by Maranello without Enzo Ferrari at the helm of the company. Introduced at the 1989 Frankfurt Motor Show, the 348 series featured a longitudinal engine with a transverse mounted gearbox. Thus the 'TB' referred to the transverse transmission Berlinetta, while the 'TS' suffix referred to transverse transmission Spider – although the 'TS' was a bit misleading as this model was more of a roadster, or 'targa' top, than a fully convertible car. The 348 Spider, a traditional Cabriolet, was launched four years later at the 1993 Geneva Motor Show.

This model signalled the introduction of the planned four-year product lifecycle (with some variances) which Ferrari had not previously followed, but which many other manufacturers were adopting. It helped with better product planning, inventory control, marketing and sales, a process that had been at best haphazard in Ferrari's early days when new models were produced almost annually, or allowed to run for up to a decade, as in the case of the 308. This can be seen in the introduction of the 328 (1985), the 348 (1989), and the 355 (1994). Similarly, the introduction of the front-engined cars followed this course in the 1990s, but more of that in the next chapter.

⟳ **A 348 TS takes shape.**
(Neill Bruce)

↥ **A 348 body shell being constructed at the Ferrari factory.** *(Neill Bruce)*

⟳ **Launched at the IAA Frankfurt Motor Show in 1989, the Ferrari 348 TB and TS took the ultra-successful 308/328 concept forward. The Ferrari 348 model inherited several Testarossa design cues, such as the simplified lateral air intake slats. The 348 was a significantly more mature package than the 328 which it replaced.**

(Motor Industry Archives)

↺ This Ferrari 348 TB, photographed at the Auto Italia day at the famous Brooklands motor circuit, shows where the next generation 355 series got its lines from – which just shows what a superbly compact and successful model the 348 was.

(Author)

The 348's larger 3404cc V8 engine developed 300bhp, but it was the styling upgrades that set this model apart. The factory once portrayed the forthcoming model as far back as 1986 as a '408 GTB', throwing any would-be sleuths off the trail by suggesting that the car was fitted with a larger 4-litre V8. In an attempt to second-guess the factory, *CAR* magazine mistakenly called the 348 a 'GTB' in their June 1988 issue, but even though they were slightly wrong on that count, they were almost dead on target with their artist's impression and technical details of the car.

With Giovanni Razelli, Ferrari's new managing director, at the helm, the new 348 would be referred to as the 'Maranello Milestone', as it incorporated many design cues from both the Testarossa and its 308/328 forebears. Although its design is unmistakably based on the 328, which it replaced, the Testarossa's air intake ducts on the doors were carried over to the 348, albeit in slightly smaller dimension. The 348 also shared the recessed front light clusters below the bumper, as well as a slightly toned down, full-width, horizontal slatted feature across the rear.

All in all, the 348 TB and TS, which were introduced simultaneously at the 1989 Frankfurt Motor Show, offered a well-styled, more rounded package than the 328 – and, with the benefit of hindsight, it more than hinted at the 355's styling, still four years away.

With their eyes firmly on the Formula 1 racing programme, Ferrari had not produced a homologated GT racer since the 288 GTO of 1984. Late in 1993 this all changed when production of the 348 GT Competizione commenced. Required to build at least 50 such cars, the Competizione was based on the standard 348 GT with the idea of qualifying a more extreme 348 in the GT3 class of international endurance racing. The GTC, as it was often referred to, was the last 348 produced by Ferrari, with 56 of these radical road cars eventually coming from Maranello, of which only eight were right-hand-drive.

↷ The perfect pair – two 348 Spiders enjoying a day out at the Ferrari Owners Club annual picnic at Wilton House, near Salisbury in Wiltshire, England. *(Author)*

➷ Cars in the park – a matching pair with a 348 Spider (left) and 348 TS (right). *(Author)*

↷➷ This rare Ferrari 348 GT Competizione is one of just eight right-hand-drive cars. *(Author)*

Back to the front

When the F355 was introduced, the improvement over its predecessor was so marked that the 328 had to make way for the newcomer.

— IAN FRASER-JONES
South African racing champion 1958—60

Ferrari in the 1990s

The 1970s and 1980s could be called Ferrari's mid-engined years, as the 308 family went from being a promising and tantalising opportunity into a fully-fledged new market sector. Without doubt, this market development provided Ferrari with a solid foundation and the financial resources to expand their product range in a way they had previously not been able to do.

To start with, this market growth would itself not have been possible without the strong brand image created by Ferrari's persistently high-profile presence on the world motor sport stage. Making great sports cars was no guarantee of success, as both Maserati and Lamborghini struggled through the 1980s and '90s, whereas Ferrari constantly moved the bar higher and higher in the supercar stakes.

Nick Mason sums it up this way, 'The others failed commercially. I mean they built great cars but then couldn't sell them. Ferrari have always had a sort of – the word 'cunning' comes to mind [laughs] – and I think also they have been lucky. The most extraordinary thing is, when it came to supercars, Ferrari managed to build something like 1,400 F40s, and sell them all.'

Ferrari's relentless motor sport programme kept their products in the limelight more than their competitors, resulting in strong sports car sales, which provided vital funding for development. 'Where there is no budget for development, you just end up knocking out the same old thing again,' Mason added.

◑ The 456 GT was Ferrari's first front-engined Grand Touring sports car with any real high-performance potential since the days of the 1968 Daytona. *(Author)*

It was this sales and sporting success that allowed Ferrari to explore the opportunity of once again producing a front-engined sports coupé. With the necessary funding, Ferrari could test new production and engineering methods, which resulted in innovative chassis and suspension developments, as well as several new engines for both front- and mid-engined configurations.

Emanuele Nicosia explains: 'The front-engined Ferrari came about as a consequence of increasing production needs and increasing models for new markets. It was decided to push the renaissance of just the mechanical layout, not [to create] a "modern" reinterpretation of 275 GTB style or some other Ferrari from the past. This meant a new design concept for a new customer, a new market segment and [therefore] new countries.'

The move to reintroduce a front-engined model into

the Ferrari family was indeed a fairly brave one, as most of the well-known supercar manufacturers in Europe and the United Kingdom had moved to the mid-engined layout because of the greater performance capabilities that this configuration offered. Admittedly, the Corvette in America, the Jaguar XJ-S, and Mercedes-Benz SL/SLC models flew the flag for the front-engined sports car sector, but somehow these were regarded as conservative Grand Tourers at best, not supercars.

So one might reasonably ask what drove Ferrari to consider a front-engined configuration again, especially as their mid-engined cars were so successful commercially. To answer this question, one should look first at what factors prompted the evolution from front-engined sports cars to mid-engined cars.

Retracing the development steps in the recent history of Ferrari sports cars, one could logically establish two distinct groups of cars – the touring-orientated front-engined 2+2 cars, such as the 400 series, and the higher performing front-engined cars, such as the 275 and Daytona. Equally interesting is the driver profile in each group, where one could fully expect to find a more mature man, possibly with a small family, buying a 400, whereas the Daytona driver was more likely to be younger and have a more sport-orientated lifestyle. Ferrari managed to create and manufacture these two product ranges simultaneously, but moving forward through the company's more recent product history, the mid-engined sports car configuration pretty much eliminated the affluent family man from the Ferrari equation, for whom a 2+2 was an attractive proposition. Ferrari didn't want to lose out on this market.

In addition, technical advances in the field of suspension and chassis developments, as well as

⌒ **An early 456 GT highlights the excellent sense of balance achieved by Pininfarina.** *(LAT)*

engine dynamics, made it possible for Ferrari's engineers to consider a move to a front-engine layout once again. Comparing some of the classic front-engined Ferraris, the Daytona was a definite two-seater and certainly more inclined towards the sporty driver. The 365 GT4 2+2 and its later 400-series derivatives, on the other hand, were clearly aimed at a different market and could be more accurately described as a classic fast gentleman's car. The 1985 Ferrari 412, the last of the 400 series, was powered by a 4943cc V12 and reached a top speed of 155mph (250kph), but the car weighed in at a hefty 1,805kg (3,979lb).

The lighter and more compact mid-engined sports car of the 1970s and '80s certainly offered some clear-cut advantages, such as greater performance and roadholding, while an important disadvantage was the absence of any back seat accommodation, and perhaps reduced luggage capacity. Sports cars are always a compromise, but the mid-engined sports car also carries a slight noise penalty with the engine being located immediately behind the passenger compartment.

However, Ferrari and Pininfarina sought to change that with the introduction of the 456 GT in 1992. In the traditional sense of the word, a Grand Tourer was the term used to describe vehicles that could participate in long distance or endurance races, such as the Le Mans 24-Hour. By definition, therefore, these cars had to be fast enough to perform on the track, but at the same time reliable and comfortable enough for long distance touring. Some of these qualities were inherited by race-inspired road cars that delivered top performance, while at the same time offering the required level of comfort for long journeys and sufficient luggage space for its

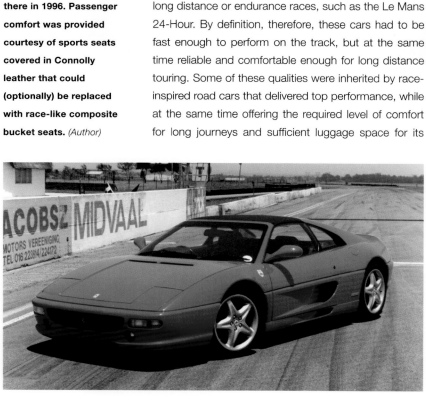

occupants. In time, through advances in automotive engineering, seating for four was made possible, as we have seen in the 365 GT4 2+2 and the subsequent 400 series.

The 456 GT changed the market's perception of a high performance 2+2 coupé by blending refinement, elegance, comfort, and performance in a Pininfarina-designed body that was both beautiful to look at and aerodynamically efficient. But the 456 GT was just one of Ferrari's new projects during the '90s, as the return of Luca di Montezemolo in 1991 served to breathe fresh life into the product range.

Nick Mason opined, 'What was interesting, of

◑ **A Ferrari F355 GTS pictured at the Midvaal circuit, south of Johannesburg, prior to a demonstration run there in 1996. Passenger comfort was provided courtesy of sports seats covered in Connolly leather that could (optionally) be replaced with race-like composite bucket seats.** *(Author)*

course, was that technology had moved on, so that in terms of roadholding you could build a very good four-seater car, which inevitably meant that the engine was at the front. I think the technical developments made this possible, but it was also to do with providing GT cars for those people in the market who wanted them.'

A year after the introduction of the 456 GT came the F355, a model that took the original 308 concept and packed it with new technology, creature comforts, and an uprated engine that gave the model a real performance edge. In fact, the F355 would become the platform that allowed Ferrari to create a one-make race series that could arguably rival the Porsche Carrera Cup series.

Mid-decade, Ferrari delivered a model to market that was unlike any other it had produced, certainly since the 1960s. The Ferrari F50 was the closest thing to a race car that the Maranello engineers could have produced, in that it incorporated Formula 1 technology and materials, and was clothed in one of the most exquisite Pininfarina-designed bodies to date. The F50 was one of those cars that would make the most indifferent motor critic stop and stare. It just shouted 'rarity', and the fact that Ferrari did not sell these cars but would only lease them to trusted and loyal customers for the first two years of 'ownership', allowed them to control who was allowed to get one.

∩ **Ferrari's F50 was one of the most radical and innovative supercars of the 1990s.** (Neill Bruce)

Luca di Montezemolo

Luca di Montezemolo returned to Ferrari in 1991 to take up the position of CEO, and immediately recognised the need to refresh the road car range. Under Montezemolo's leadership, Ferrari progressed with the launch of one successful product after the other, starting with the 456 GT, followed by the F355, the F50 and the magnificent 550 Maranello, while the 360 Modena rounded off a fruitful and very busy decade.

⚲ Luca di Montezemolo was passionate about Ferrari's Formula 1 team. Here he monitors their progress at the track in 1992. *(Ferrari SpA)*

Montezemolo's influence brought Ferrari flying into the 21st century, with radical models such as the Enzo, and later the FXX, while the F430 replaced the 360 series. Further front-engined models (612 Scaglietti, 599 GTB, and the later Superamerica and California) pushed the boundaries of excellence and progress.

Started in 1997, Montezemolo's visionary 'Formula Uomo' concept, a 200-million-Euro corporate investment, transformed the company and its working environment, turning the Ferrari facility into a beautiful, ecologically smart 'village' devoted to constructing cars of the highest technology. Translated practically, if not literally, 'Formula Uomo' means 'Formula People', with the prime objective of transforming the Maranello plant into a state-of-the-art manufacturing and working environment. If they claimed to produce the best sports cars in the world, then they needed a modern facility that looked the part, and where the company and its employees could feel they were moving into the future and writing their own history.

Upon the death of Fiat's then Chairman, Umberto Agnelli, Luca di Montezemolo was appointed Chairman of Fiat S.p.A., Ferrari's parent company, in 2004.

The 1996 Ferrari 550 Maranello saw the re-emergence of a model which was surely the modern-day equivalent of the 1968 Daytona. Ferrari's continuing expansion into the front-engined GT market took a big step forward with this model, which once again gave the company an excellent foothold in the GT endurance racing world.

In the words of Sergio Pininfarina, technological progress in the '90s meant that a mid-engine was no longer necessary for a car to achieve top performance. The return to the front-engine configuration was a deliberate decision on the part of Ferrari, as this format offered a spacious, comfortable cabin and a large luggage compartment, which enabled much wider use of the car. Ferrari's front-engined supercars of the 1990s were all a blend of innovation, functionality, comfort, and performance. Catering for the modern sports car buyer also required the provision of many electronic driving aids and interior comforts, and the 456 and 550 models served once again to lift Ferrari into the realm of the high-performance luxury Grand Tourer.

Ferrari 512 TR (1992) and F512 M (1994)

Reviving the Testarossa concept of the 1980s, Ferrari reintroduced its 'Boxer' model in the form of the 512 TR, launched in Los Angeles in 1992. In the wake of the now long-in-the-tooth Testarossa (1984–91), Ferrari perhaps could not bear to be without a large-capacity 12-pot boxer-engined supercar in its range.

Although this model retained many of the Testarossa's familiar features, such as the slatted side air intakes and rear light treatment, it now featured a revised, more rounded front end (similar to the 348), which included a more defined grille and a body-coloured front lip.

Introduced at the 1994 Paris Motor Show was the final evolution of the Testarossa, the F512 M ('M' for Modificato). The visual gap between the F512 M and its immediate predecessor, the 512 TR, was far greater than the difference between the original Testarossa and the 512 TR.

Although the general shape of the F512 M remained very similar to the TR and the Testarossa, there were several styling differences in the latest version that set it apart. Gone were the pop-up headlamps, these being replaced by ellipsoidal lights set behind clear glass. The nose section was further refined with a smaller grille made possible by better air intake management, while

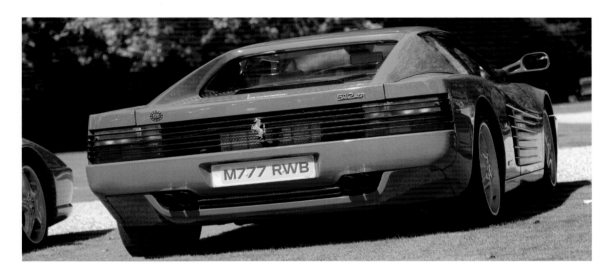

↻ Ferrari's 512 TR carried the legendary Testarossa's blood in its veins. *(Author)*

↺ The Testarossa concept was finally terminated with the powerful F512 M, a truly awesome package, but with some mixed styling, such as the front end with its exposed headlamps and 348-style grille. *(Author)*

↻ 'Wide' is perhaps the first word that comes to mind here, but the F512 M's rear track was actually slightly narrower than the Testarossa on which it was based. *(Author)*

separate light units were recessed into the bodywork making for an altogether new look. The full-width slatted cover over the rear lights (which had previously covered rectangular light clusters) made way for new twin round light units, but the slats remained in the middle to aid engine cooling.

Ferrari 456 GT (1992)

Ferrari's front-engined sports cars had been steadily losing ground to their mid-engined siblings, and the company were keen to ensure their new four-seater coupé was a match for its two-seat models. Introduced at the Paris Motor Show in October 1992, the basic philosophy behind the 456 GT was a fusion of the performance and driving pleasure of a supercar, combined with the comfort, space and practicality of a four-seater vehicle. Around this concept, Pininfarina sculptured a body that was aggressive while remaining compact and aerodynamic, but at the same time successfully retaining overall dimensions similar to a classic two-seater.

To combine aggressiveness, a streamlined body, and supreme comfort in a supercar is some challenge, for they are not easy bedfellows. As already stated, a sports car is all about compromise. But in the 456 GT, Pininfarina succeeded in marrying these elements to produce a most harmonious supercar, which was capable, according to the manufacturer, of a top speed of over 186mph (300kph) while accommodating four adults. Such performance would ordinarily only be achievable in a stripped-out, highly-tuned supercar fitted with racing seats and track suspension.

Although the 456 GT was Ferrari's first front-engined road car since the demise of the 412 in 1985, it was a full 25 years since the introduction of its closest four-seat relative, the 365 GT 2+2 back in 1967. Based on looks alone, the 456 shares design cues from a range of Ferrari road cars, both historical and contemporary.

Being a front-engined road car, the larger grille size indicates the use of a single front-mounted radiator. The position and location of the narrow V-angle, large-capacity engine mounted in the chassis is well disguised

○ Classic long bonnet and short boot proportions helped to give this 1994 Ferrari 456 GT 2+2 excellent balance and handling. *(Neill Bruce)*

○ Seating for four adults with luggage space to match made the Ferrari 456 GT 2+2 a practical sports car, albeit with supercar performance. *(Neill Bruce)*

when looking at the low forward-sloping bonnet line. The nose is a pleasing combination of functionality and elegance, with Ferrari's trademark pop-up headlamps located in the wings (fenders), while the low-level driving lights are found embedded in the attractive, oval grille.

Immediately behind the front wheel-arches, and hinting at its massive performance, are the hot air exit vents for the massive 5474cc V12 engine, and this has been incorporated into an attractive and eye-catching, streamlined 'swish' feature on each flank. For a four-seat supercar, able to accommodate four adults, the 456 has a remarkably low roofline (1,300mm/51in compared to the 348 TB's 1,170mm/46in), forming a continuous arc from the windscreen's leading edge to the tip of the boot lid, with the line descending gracefully towards the back giving a very 'Daytona' look from the rear view.

The 456 has a very 'full' look, in that all surfaces are convex to maximise interior space, and by this method Pininfarina ensured that the car could carry four adults, although a transcontinental journey in the back of a 456 might be quite challenging for a pair of adults. There is not an angry panel on the 456, and it epitomised the successful execution of a mature design right from day one. The 456 GTA featured an automatic transmission for those who wanted a slightly easier life.

But the aerodynamics of the 456 are not down to good design alone, as this four-seater supercar spent much of its development time in the windtunnel having its underbody defined. An innovative and critical feature of the aero package involved a retractable flap under the rear bumper that was electronically controlled in accordance with the speed of the vehicle, thereby reducing rear axle lift at speed. This spoiler was an integral part of the rear aerodynamic profile of the 456, while the front spoiler reduced front axle lift and improved airflow towards the rear.

One might also say that the 456 was a powerhouse of new technology, and this description could be applied to the body assembly process as well. The 456 GT's light aluminium bodywork was spot-welded to its steel chassis by means of an innovative steel foil (Feran) that allowed the two different metals to be welded together, forming a very rigid structure. Further exotic materials, comprising a sandwich composite with a honeycomb layer, were used on the bonnet and the retractable headlamp covers to achieve rigidity without adding weight. The frameless door windows lowered automatically during the opening and closing of the door, a feature common on many coupés today, but quite advanced at the time the Ferrari 456 GT was produced.

Even now the 456 still cuts a purposeful look, but in its day it was simply stunning. The elegant and distinctive interior was fitted with exquisite Connolly leather and fine woods, not far removed from the traditional finish one might expect to find inside certain British luxury marques. The front accommodation was impressive to say the least, and rear passengers could travel in reasonable comfort provided journeys were relatively short. There was no list of options, as the 456 came with a full house of extras, even down to the five-piece fitted leather luggage set.

The Ferrari 456 GT could quite possibly go down as the best looking 2+2 of all time.

Ferrari F355 (1994)

Ian Fraser-Jones, South African motor racing champion from 1958 to 1960, had always been a 'Porsche man', until he discovered Ferrari. He had his first chance to do just that in 1981, and realised immediately that he was sitting in a race-bred car – the 308. It wasn't long before he acquired his own 308, which he owned for five years before replacing it with the 328.

'However, when the F355 was introduced, the improvement over its predecessor was so marked that the 328 had to make way for the newcomer. With 110bhp more than the 328 and only an 85kg penalty, the performance advantage of the F355 was staggering (263–295kph),' Fraser-Jones commented.

Tracing its bloodline back through the 348 and the 328 to the 308 of 1975, the F355 had a lot to live up to,

⟲ **An early F355 coupé, or Berlinetta, poses in a typical Italian village during the press drive – the contrast between old and new is striking.** *(LAT)*

as sales of its predecessors had been strong. After all, it was the iconic 308 GTB that had for Ferrari cemented the niche mid-engined market, then in its infancy, but the F355 was now the newcomer that would have to establish the platform from which the next generation of compact Ferrari sports cars would be launched.

Sergio Pininfarina regarded the F355 as one of the best Ferraris ever built. With a top speed of 183mph (295kph) from its naturally-aspirated 3.5-litre V8 engine, performance was even better than its athletic appearance suggested, thanks to its superb aerodynamic efficiency and underbody design which was optimised following an in-depth ground-effect analysis.

The author can recall the 100-plus kilometre drive from Johannesburg to the Midvaal circuit with owner Ian Fraser-Jones and commenting on how much Ferrari had changed in terms of sophisticated electronic

driving aids – he agreed with me. There were air bags and buttons for the fully-adjustable driver's seat, and height-adjustable steering wheel, electric mirrors, air-conditioning, suspension and shock absorber settings, all controlled from within the cockpit – a far cry from Ferrari sports cars of the 1950s. But Ferrari, like all other sportscar manufacturers, had to move with the times and keep apace with their customers' expectations.

The Ferrari F355 Berlinetta and Targa-topped GTS burst on to the scene at the Geneva Motor Show in spring 1994. Styled, once again, by Pininfarina, the F355 inherited many characteristics from its 308/328/348 predecessors, blending them in a subtle balance of aerodynamics and aesthetics that focused on simplicity and unity of form. Gone were the multiple slats filling the side-mounted radiator intakes, as well as the full-width blades covering the rear light clusters, the overall F355 styling instead being more rounded and pleasing to the eye. In fact, the overall body shape was almost identical to the outgoing 348, but despite being fractionally longer and wider (to accommodate wider rubber), the F355 was slightly lighter.

Although the F355 was dimensionally slightly larger than the 348, it was aerodynamically more efficient, thanks to the endless hours spent testing in the windtunnel. Aerodynamic development focused on attaining a good coefficient of negative lift (Cz) without the addition of unnecessary exterior styling elements. The front spoiler incorporated air intakes for the brake discs, while being shaped to optimise and smooth the underbody airflow which exited through the integrated

⊃ Along with the F355 GTS badging on the tail of this Ferrari is another significant emblem signifying that the car's owner is a member of the 'Club International des Anciens Pilotes de Grand Prix'. Membership of this exclusive club requires one to have competed successfully in a Grand Prix during the 'golden days', and as Ian Fraser-Jones won the 1960 Grand Prix Adriatique, he was well qualified to join the likes of Moss, Fangio, Hill, and others. *(Author)*

⊃ Close inspection of the rear lip of the engine cover reveals the nolder that Ferrari developed for the F355, designed to improve airflow over the rear bodywork. *(Author)*

outlets in the car's rear diffuser. Cooling air for the engine's side-mounted radiators and rear brakes was channelled through the more rounded intakes in the doors and sill (rocker panel).

The rear end of the F355 incorporated a discreet engine cover lip, called a nolder (Ferrari describe this as 'a small protuberance along the edge of the tail') similar to the 348 but further developed, while the extremely short body overhang enhanced airflow and grip. For the coupé version, the badging simply read 'F355 berlinetta' or 'F355 GTS' for the Targa-topped model.

Three F355 derivatives were introduced in 1995 – the Spider, Challenge, and 355 Competizione. The F355 Spider convertible broke cover on Rodeo Drive in Beverly Hills and was the first Ferrari to feature an electronically-controlled power top. The Ferrari F355 Challenge, which was produced to compete in Ferrari's popular Challenge Series, weighed in at approximately 200lb (about 90kg) less than the street car. The 355 Competizione featured a Formula 1 gearbox and adjustable rear wing, and was approximately 500lb (about 227kg) lighter than the F355 Berlinetta.

⋂ Ferrari F355 Berlinetta – an extremely athletic-looking sports car with excellent poise, a wide stance, and strong lines. *(Author)*

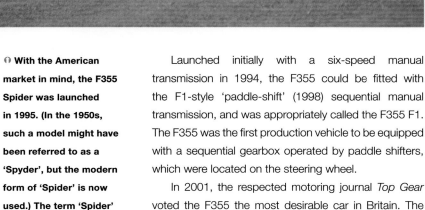

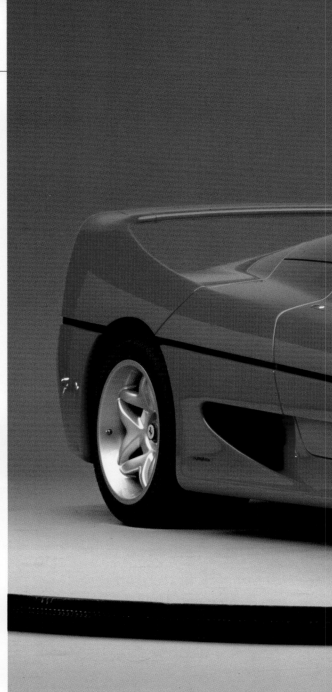

Launched initially with a six-speed manual transmission in 1994, the F355 could be fitted with the F1-style 'paddle-shift' (1998) sequential manual transmission, and was appropriately called the F355 F1. The F355 was the first production vehicle to be equipped with a sequential gearbox operated by paddle shifters, which were located on the steering wheel.

In 2001, the respected motoring journal *Top Gear* voted the F355 the most desirable car in Britain. The magazine revealed that while there might have been faster Ferraris, and perhaps some better-looking Ferraris in the past, there had not been a better balanced and more rewarding model to drive.

Ferrari F50 (1995)

Why was the 1995 Geneva Motor Show one to remember? It was the venue selected by Ferrari for the launch of the F50, the successor to the F40, and the flag-bearer of Maranello's model range. The F50 was not fitted with Ferrari's biggest engine to date, nor did it carry any turbochargers, but it was a smidgen quicker than the F40, making it the fastest road car Ferrari had ever built.

For some time, loyal customers had been pressuring Ferrari to once again build a V12-engined supercar to replace the F40 with its V8, as these Ferraristi felt that a true Ferrari Berlinetta should be unturbocharged and have twelve cylinders rather than eight. The development path

of the F50 from the drawing board to the road was a long one, and one filled with many curves, but the final product was just what Piero Ferrari, the company's vice president, had wanted right from the start – a road-going supercar as close to a Formula 1 car as was legally possible.

The F40 had been a fast, extreme looking, no-holds-barred all-out sports car, but the F50 needed to be better. Where the F40 had used the 288 GTO's mechanicals as its starting point, the F50 prototype started its career with actual Formula 1 suspension components and an engine derived directly from Alain Prost's 641/2 1990 Formula 1 car. It was important to Ferrari that the passion of Formula 1 racing was bred into the F50 right from

the drawing board stage, well before its wheels even touched the ground. Production numbers were carefully worked out, and it was agreed that 350 cars would be the production ceiling, but in keeping with Enzo Ferrari's methods, the final quantity would be fixed at 349, just one car less than the market could absorb (according to the factory), in order to ensure strong demand.

In celebration of 50 years of Ferrari's car-making activities, the F50, codenamed F130 inside the factory, needed to be very special. Where the F40's Kevlar and fibreglass body was built around a tubular steel trellis chassis, the F50 had to replicate the Formula 1 car's carbon fibre fabricated tub and bodywork. The weight

◠ **The F50's styling was revolutionary, quite unlike anything the company had produced to date.** *(LAT)*

differential between the two was a miniscule 11lb (5kg), with the F40 being the heavier of the two at 2,723lb (1,235kg). Prototype test drivers included Niki Lauda, Jean Alesi, and Gerhard Berger, and while it was never intended to race the F50, the overall shape of the car was also modelled on the Group C racers of the day.

Much of the inspiration for the F50 came from Pininfarina's 1989 Mythos concept car which was first revealed to the public at the Tokyo Motor Show in October of that year. Early F50 designs showed the car with a sharp, pointed chin spoiler, a feature that, thankfully, was revised on the final model. Although Ferrari's initial intention was to create two models, a coupé and a spider, a decision to combine these two aspects in one vehicle was taken fairly late into the project's development – a move that undoubtedly had a significant impact on the strong appeal of the final production car. Thus the F50 was both a Berlinetta and a Barchetta, being changed by the owner from one to the other as the need arose. However, removing the roof panel was not a simple task, as some found out after scratching the rather prone interchangeable roof sections.

Constructed entirely from carbon fibre, the swooping body of the F50 is dynamic and efficient from any angle. The front body section contains twin radiator outlets, which initially caused some problems as the hot radiator air would wash uncomfortably over the occupants, until small winglets were added to the A-pillars. The back end was characterised by a large spoiler (initially intended to be adjustable but ultimately left in a fixed position to prevent enthusiastic owners meddling with the F50's aerodynamics) that provided critical downforce at the top end. The factory gave the F50's drag coefficient as 0.372, which was extremely good for a supercar with such downforce capabilities.

The twin humps behind the F50's occupants cleverly concealed sturdy roll-over hoops, and this was stylishly incorporated into the overall design of the car. The flanks were characterised by Ferrari's large traditional air intakes, which fed the brakes and enhanced airflow through the engine bay. Pininfarina also incorporated a swage line, or scalfatura, which ran the full length of the car from the radiator grille in the front to the rear light clusters. This served to visually split the car, breaking up the large surface area towards the rear, and it also added to the car's streamlined appearance.

➲ **Dramatic but elegant would describe the Ferrari F50. There was no mistaking what model this was, with its high, swooping rear wing arrangement.** *(Neill Bruce)*

The front splitter was slightly raised in the centre to allow air to pass under the car, which was protected by a full-width, full-length undertray and culminated in twin tunnels at the rear, all of which contributed to the F50's superb aerodynamics.

While this book's main concern is design, one cannot mention the F50 without referring to the car's phenomenal performance. Where the F40's twin-turbocharged 2.9-litre V8 pushed out 478bhp and could do the 0–62mph (0–100kph) sprint in 4.1sec, the F50 on the other hand was fitted with a V12 of 4.7-litre capacity and developed 513bhp which helped it to a 0–62mph (0–100kph) time of 3.87sec. The F50 went on to a top speed of 202mph (325kph), staggering by anyone's measure.

Where Jaguar (XJ220), Bugatti (EB110), and McLaren (F1) had struggled to sell their supercars in the early 1990s, Ferrari could have trebled their production of the F50 and probably sold the lot without any difficulty.

U The F50 could be converted into an open-top 'roadster' by removing the roof, although this was not a simple matter. The humps behind the seats which housed the roll-over bars served to add a streamlining effect to the rear bodywork, as well as adding strength to the car. *(LAT)*

In the mid-1980s, the F40's initial production was fixed at 400 prior to Enzo's death, but when values soared, Ferrari ramped up production to a whopping 1,337 and had no difficulty in selling all of these cars during its production life, which stretched from 1987 to 1992.

But Ferrari made it absolutely clear that under no circumstances would they increase their initial production of the F50, as that would undermine the trust of those who had shelled out £329,000 for a unique slice of history. There was talk of producing a limited quantity of F50 race cars to compete in the GT class, and tests were indeed carried out by test driver Dario Benuzzi, but the project was terminated without any further work being done.

In its time, the Ferrari F50 was a triumph of desire, function, and form. Many years later, the F50 is still held in awe, and it will continue to extract the same reaction from young and old alike, just as the 250 GTO and Daytona do today. That makes the F50 a landmark car.

↷ An F50 press car is put through its paces at Fiorano, Ferrari's test track at the factory. *(LAT)*

↳ Taken during the car's introduction to the media at Fiorano, this rear three-quarter shot of the F50 highlights the dominant size and proportion of the rear spoiler (wing) and its sweeping side supports. *(LAT)*

Ferrari 550 Maranello (1996)

The Ferrari 550 Maranello press kit explained the brief given to the Ferrari engineers: 'Design and build a car able to meet the needs of Ferrari customers looking for driving emotions and exciting performance, who do not want to forego driveability or comfort.'

This brief covered factors such as the car's performance, quality of 'life onboard', and a styling efficiency that connected the modern interpretation of this brief with Ferrari's traditional sporting heritage. The result was a front-engined sports coupé that could lap Ferrari's Fiorano track 3.2sec quicker than the mid-engined 512 supercar.

The aerodynamic shape of the 550 Maranello, named in recognition of the town in which Ferrari has its home, was the result of 4,800 hours of work in the windtunnel. This level of research was necessary in order to achieve the design targets set for the car, namely:

- Constant vertical load on the wheels, irrespective of vehicle set-up;
- Minimal sensitivity to side winds;
- Minimal drag (Cd=0.33).

In particular, the vertical load independent of set-up combined with a coefficient of lift (Cz) lower than zero is a unique achievement for a car with no adjustable body elements or added aerodynamic surfaces (such as a separate aerodynamic foil or wing). Particular care went into the design of the front of the car, the aerodynamic efficiency of the air intakes, and the interior airflows.

It is fair to say that Pininfarina's design for this Berlinetta is an extreme interpretation of the classic front-engined sports coupé for which Ferrari had

꩜ **The new Ferrari 550 Maranello was launched at the Paris Motor Show in October 1996.** *(Motor Industry Archives)*

꩜ **Caught in a peaceful Italian village on the occasion of the 550's press launch.** *(LAT)*

The 550 featured a pair of inclined air vents on the flanks just ahead of the doors, a feature that has its roots in the front-engined Ferraris of the 1950s. Large, muscular rear haunches gave the car a dynamic stance.

(LAT)

become so well known in earlier years. Replacing the F50 as Maranello's flagship model, the 550 was not just a blisteringly quick sports car, it also set new standards of luxury in that segment of the market, and it did so while reviving a deep tradition in Ferrari lore, while creating a modern front-engined supercar in the process.

Pininfarina's classic long bonnet/short boot design immediately gave the 550 a traditional Ferrari sports car silhouette. However, the 550 could not just be a brawny, big-engined supercar, it had to satisfy certain strict criteria such as not being too ostentatious, but comprising more sober and functional lines which were in keeping with market requirements of the day. The 550 also needed to

satisfy the widest possible range of uses that the owner might subject it to, which would include both city and motorway use, and possible track day adventures. Most important, the 550 needed to reflect the considerable styling heritage that Ferrari's front-engined sports cars had created over the years.

The wide rear track enabled the designers to create high and broad rear shoulders giving a powerful look to the car's rear end. The slender roof pillars and relatively light greenhouse sitting atop a chunky body lowers the optical centre of gravity, and serves to magnify the impression of power and speed.

The long bonnet features a large functional intake vent which feeds air to the engine, an engineering

requirement that linked the present with the past. The two exit vents, sitting between the front wheel-arch and the door, allow hot engine air to escape, and are angled forward (at the top edge) creating the perception of speed and elegance. These technical apertures are typical of Ferrari's styling from as far back as the 1950s (as seen on the 1953 Ferrari 250 MM and 375 MM, and the immortal 1962 250 GTO), but they also performed an important functional role.

The car's volumes are clean and frank and not smoothed or tapered, thus creating a full, muscular body marked by dihedral lines that dominate the larger surfaces. These dihedrons serve to highlight the car's lines and add to its overall character and presence.

The nose of the 550 came in for much attention, as it was a requirement that the car generated zero front-end lift, but at the same time the engineers had to ensure a family resemblance with earlier sports cars. This is the first Ferrari since the 1960s to have been conceived and designed from the start with visible front light clusters integrated into the shape of the bonnet and wing line. The thinking behind this was that it would improve the car's aerodynamic efficiency during night driving, and would reduce wind noise. The main air intake grille was purposely located lower and incorporated the fog lights, while the complex lower leading edge of the splitter was integrated into the overall aero package to optimise the 550's streamlining.

⌒ **Ferrari's typical front-engined sports car proportions are highlighted in this overhead view of the 550 Maranello. Pop-up headlamps had been replaced by visible light clusters, and the rather menacing bonnet air intake created the impression of power.** (LAT)

↺↻ Launched a full four years after the Berlinetta, the strikingly beautiful 550 Barchetta was certainly a handsome addition to the 550 family. *(Author)*

Those who thought that the 550 was just a jazzed up 456 couldn't be more wrong, as apart from sharing the same basic engine there were few similarities. While it had a much wider track front and rear, and was therefore a good deal wider overall, the 550 sat on a shorter wheelbase and was around 8in (208mm) shorter and about 1in (23mm) lower than the four-seater 456, further highlighting the car's muscular proportions. The tail was also shorter and featured an upswept aerodynamic lip, which increased downforce at speed. Weighing the same as the 456 at 3,726lb (1,690kg) and with 40bhp more under the bonnet, the 550 boasted a top speed of 200mph (320kph).

Not unlike the Daytona, the 550 featured twin round optical clusters at the rear and a quad exhaust system. Fitted with traction control, the 550 was, in short, an astonishingly quick sports car, and equipped with the highest quality interior fittings to boot. Just as the Daytona had been, back in 1968, the Ferrari 550 was aimed at the discerning gentleman driver with a sporty character.

The 550 Barchetta Pininfarina (only 448 produced), to which Ferrari had given the name Pininfarina for the first time on the occasion of that company's 70th anniversary, was presented at the Mondial de l'Automobile 2000 in Paris. The aim of the design and development team was to offer a unique interpretation along the lines of the purest Ferrari specials, which meant going for a deliberately provocative look to make it stand out from the standard product range.

The launch of the 575M Maranello at the 72nd Geneva International Motor Show (2002) marked a significant milestone for Ferrari as the latest iteration of the iconic 12-cylinder, front-engined Berlinetta. The evolution of the 575M Maranello took the 550 concept to a new level, representing the extreme expression of a front-engined Ferrari Berlinetta in terms of superb technical and performance capability.

On 4 July 2002 the 575M Maranello ('M' stands for Modificato or Modified) was launched in the United Kingdom. Featuring a 5748cc version of the 550's V12 engine, the new model only featured minor exterior upgrades, mostly in the area of better cooling (larger front air intakes) and downforce (full-width front chin spoiler). With power output increased to 515bhp, the 575M's top speed was a staggering 202mph (325kph). Weight distribution was now a perfect 50/50 split with driver on board.

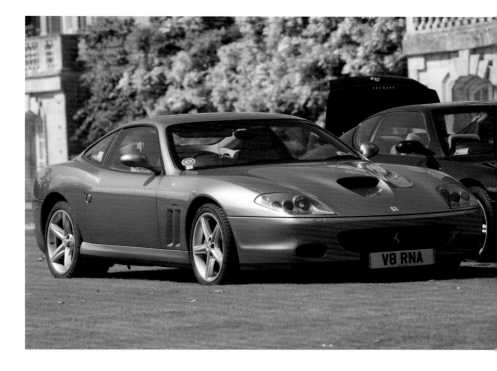

⌒ Outwardly it was quite difficult to distinguish between the 575M and its older 550 sibling, but one point to compare is the lower front brake cooling ducts which, on the newer car, were slightly larger and further out. *(Author)*

⌒ The 575M Maranello featured the same pert boot lip as the 550. *(Author)*

Ferrari 360 Modena (1999)

The end of a century is surely a good enough reason to create a new Ferrari, and the 360 Modena, named after the town where Enzo first set up the Ferrari name, was to be the company's millennium car. Now boasting a larger 3.6-litre V8 engine, the 360 Modena was set to replace the F355 that had laid the foundation for Ferrari's sports cars for the new millennium.

Code-named the F131, the 360 Modena accounted for almost two-thirds of all Ferrari's production, and therefore it was imperative that the new model should provide real world usability. A challenge was that, while reducing weight by a massive 34 per cent, the body size had to be increased to meet market demands for greater comfort and higher equipment levels.

Ferrari's Project Manager, Maurizio Manfredini, had overall responsibility for the 360 project, which was a complete redesign from scratch of the mid-engine concept using a stiffer all-aluminium chassis and bodyshell, a first for a Ferrari road car. This clean-sheet redesign enabled the engineers to retain the car's weight at 2,976lb (1,350kg) – the same as the F355 – but the 360 was longer, wider, and higher than its predecessor.

The body dimensions show how the overall shape of the car had changed from a narrower front-to-rear track measurement on the F355 to the narrower rear-to-front track dimensions of the 360. The longer wheelbase offered a smoother ride, and with shorter body overhangs front and rear, the 360 enjoyed a negative lift coefficient

⊃ **The Ferrari 360 Modena featured a much more aggressive front end with larger air intake ducts. This is the Modena F1 variant with electrohydraulic gear change.** *(Neill Bruce)*

Ferrari F355 and 360 Modena body dimensions comparison

Dimension	F355 (1995)	360 Modena (1999)
Wheelbase (mm)	2,450	2,600
Track front/rear (mm)	1,514/1,615	1,669/1,617
Length (mm)	4,250	4,477
Width (mm)	1,900	1,922
Height (mm)	1,170	1,235
Kerb weight (kg)	1,350	1,350

Source: Ferrari press kits

(Cz). Although the 360 was an altogether better car, both aerodynamically and technically, it had somehow lost some of the innocence and naivety that the earlier mid-engined 3-series Ferraris had enjoyed. Where the compact-styled 308, 328, 348, and 355 had been both smaller and more pleasing to the eye, the 360 was a more in-your-face design that shouted its presence to all the world through its very vocal-looking front end.

Around 5,400 hours in the windtunnel produced several front end improvements over the F355, namely twin air intakes for the radiators, which replaced the large single intake on the earlier model. The radiator venting was positioned just ahead of the front wheels, thereby creating a unique treatment for this function on a Ferrari sports car. Instead of the customary pop-up headlamps, the 360 featured smaller exposed light clusters in the front wings (fenders) located behind clear covers, which further contributed to the car's aerodynamic efficiency.

As a carry-over from the Formula 1 programme, the 360's smooth underbody comprised a virtual tunnel created by the centrally raised front splitter section that exits at the rear through twin extractors. This development ensures smooth airflow, preventing a build-up of air under the car and thereby creating the negative

Cz factor, and a drag coefficient of 0.335 (Cd). This is where Ferrari has been able to transfer its aerodynamic lessons, learned on the track in their Formula 1 cars, to the road-going GT cars. But it is not just a matter of transferring directly all the findings on to the road car, as this would make the car difficult and uncomfortable to drive for long periods. The study of fluid dynamics has helped greatly to ensure that the GT road cars are both pleasing to look at and technically efficient from an aerodynamic perspective.

Road cars are, therefore, a compromise as there are no exterior adjustable parts such as those on a Formula 1 race car. So, getting the aero package right is essential for these reasons. At 180mph (290kph) the 360's body generates almost 400lb (180kg) of downforce, which is astonishing for a sports car devoid of exterior adjustable aerodynamic aids.

The absence of any adjustable wings ensured a clean and simple body line. Cooling intake vents on the rear wings are reminiscent of the 250 LM race car, and channel air to the engine (left) and oil radiator (right). Placing these prominent intakes on the rear 'shoulders' serves to enhance the car's muscular appearance, just as it did on the 250 LM back in 1963.

⌒ A carbon fibre rear grille was fitted as standard on the 360 Challenge cars, but many 360 owners chose to retrofit these on their road cars, replacing the standard body-coloured panel. This upgrade was then offered by the factory as an optional extra on normal 360 road cars which proved popular since it was a straight swap. *(Author)*

⋃ The 360 Modena offered an aerodynamically efficient and yet simple and pleasing design. Lateral venting on the 360 was quite different from its predecessor, the F355, in that the two radiators were placed ahead of the front axle, resulting in exit vents ahead of the front wheels. Engine intakes were mounted along the sills (rocker panels) as well as high up on the rear shoulders. *(Author)*

The air intakes ahead of the rear wheels ventilate the engine bay with air, which is then extracted through the low-pressure area created around the grilles either side of the rear windscreen and through the cut-outs in the rear bumper.

From the side, a swage line, which starts from the front wing below the light cluster, continues along the full length of the car, rising towards the rear and creating a wedge-like style, thereby giving the impression of speed. The passenger compartment is almost perfectly centrally located, ensuring excellent mid-engined sports car performance and ride. An extremely low-angled rear windscreen not only enhances the flow of air over the rear bodywork, but it also allows the heart of the Ferrari, its V8 engine, to be permanently on display. The rear end

⊂ **Launched a year after the 360 Modena, the 360 Spider (no 'Modena') lost none of its performance or aerodynamic efficiency and in fact weighed the same as its Berlinetta sibling.** *(Author)*

⊍ **Designed by Pininfarina, the introduction of the 360 Spider marked this company's 70th anniversary. The Spider's graceful design was a fitting tribute to Pininfarina's continued creativity.** *(Author)*

is traditional Ferrari, with twin round tail lights either side, harking back to early 1960s styling.

Although the 360 Spider debuted at the 2000 Geneva Motor Show, it had been part of the 360 project from the outset. However, the alternative of a Barchetta model always poses additional challenges not encountered with the Berlinetta, and not only on issues relating to body rigidity. When it concerns a Ferrari sports cars, adherence to traditional design and styling criteria are essential, and that means efficient hood folding and stowage, as this affects the car's aerodynamic efficiency.

Pininfarina celebrated 70 years in business with the launch of the 360 Spider, with almost 50 of those years as Ferrari's prime design house, a remarkable achievement by any standards.

As a result of extensive body research, the Pininfarina designers accomplished a Cd of 0.36 for the Spider (against the Modena's 0.335) while the overall downforce was slightly lower at 374lb (170kg) against almost 400lb (180kg) for the Berlinetta. This was achieved partly through the incorporation of a nolder on the trailing edge of the rear engine cover lip. This overall aerodynamic achievement in itself is quite remarkable, because the airflow over the roof of the Spider was significantly disrupted owing to the hood shape and the stowage

requirements, which demanded some clever redesign work in the area immediately behind the rear window. With the hood stowed, the open Spider appeared to have borrowed some design cues from the F50 with its twin humps behind the occupants, an observation confirmed when viewing the car from the front three-quarter angle.

⌒ **Increased power, reduced weight, lowered suspension, and electrohydraulic gear change was standard in Ferrari's 360 Challenge Stradale.** (Author)

⌒ **The glorious engine of the Ferrari 360 Challenge Stradale is visible to all, and why not! From the outset, Ferrari engineers designed the car with an 80/20 road-to-track usage ratio in mind, and it is 243lb (110kg) lighter than the standard 360 Modena.** (Author)

➲ Ready for the 2000 season, the 360 Challenge differed from the road-going Modena only in certain details, which included a custom Challenge grille, larger 18in BBS alloys, and a slightly lower ride height. The 400bhp 3586cc V8 was left untouched and was supplied to the teams sealed, just as Porsche did with their Carrera Cup cars. The F1 gearbox, which allowed lightning-quick gear changes (150 milliseconds) was fitted to all Challenge cars. *(Author)*

Front-engine dominance

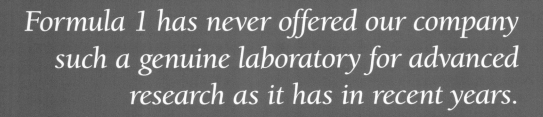

*Formula 1 has never offered our company
such a genuine laboratory for advanced
research as it has in recent years.*

— LUCA DI MONTEZEMOLO
Ferrari President

Ferrari in the new millennium

In recent years, Ferrari sports cars have moved away from that big, brutish image of power and muscle, with specific reference to the iconic 250 models and the Daytona of 1968, towards a more sophisticated driving package encompassing power steering, power accessories, and many electronic driver aids.

Nick Mason agrees: 'You are absolutely right. First of all, I don't think there is room for any bad cars [in the market] anymore, everyone has to make good cars now, it's too global to be able to get away with anything that isn't pretty terrific. But I also think that under Luca, after the "Old Man" died, in a way the company sort of leapt forward in terms of embracing modern technology and utilising all the available expertise.'

It was necessary for Ferrari to embrace this new generation of technology and sophistication, as the cars from Maranello had to compete in an increasingly congested market. Even Ferrari had unfairly suffered from the reputation of unreliability that had hung over the Italian motor industry for years, and this was a shadow which Luca di Montezemolo was determined to step out of.

'You know, it was actually quite acceptable to have a car that didn't start back in the '60s [laughs], and you always knew a man around the corner called "Luigi" who would come and change 24 plugs for you before you headed out. But Ferrari knew, quite rightly, that they were competing with Porsche, and the one thing that Porsche was going to be was ultra-reliable. So, in order to keep up, Ferrari had to get that part of the package absolutely right,' added Mason.

The first year of the new century was undoubtedly the year of the Spiders, the first being the 360 Spider introduced at Geneva in March, while the 550 Barchetta Pininfarina was announced at the Paris show that same year.

However, Ferrari's intentions were not to be limited to the soft tops aimed at the boulevard cruisers, as the introduction of models such as the mid-engined Enzo and F430 models would testify, while the 612 Scaglietti and 599 GTB Fiorano would bolster Maranello's front-engined regiment. Both technical and market requirements pointed to the need for a new generation of front-engined grand tourers.

The second half of the decade would see the introduction of two new models that would rekindle the iconic names of Superamerica and California. These two open-top sports cars were clearly aimed at reinforcing the name of Ferrari amongst the well-heeled movie stars and celebrities of Hollywood where some of Maranello's most prized products tended to find a home.

Between the years 1994 and 2004, Ferrari driver Michael Schumacher would rewrite the Formula 1 record books by taking the World Championship no fewer than seven times in eleven years, with an unprecedented five consecutive titles between 2000 and 2004. Did this have any influence on Ferrari's success in the showrooms? You bet it did. The Scuderia's achievements were talked about at boardroom and dining room tables, and in homes around the world by housewives and most children, right up to the age of 90 and more. The name Ferrari was splashed across newspapers and in magazines in every nation, and the immeasurable marketing success of this story was that more people than ever were talking about the sport and, importantly, the Ferrari brand. Riding the crest of a big popularity wave, Ferrari moved to brand everything from ski boots and skateboards to mouse pads and teddy bears, which appeared in boutique shops across the globe from California to China. No doubt there will be differing opinions as to the value that this adds to the world's most celebrated sports car brand.

◑ With a top speed of 192mph (310kph), Ferrari's F430 Spider took open-top motoring to new levels. Although such speed may never be experienced by most owners of this super-quick rag-top, the author can testify that performance in this sports car is scintillating. *(Author)*

↷ Although it was launched in 2004, Ferrari still showed the 612 Scaglietti at the 2008 Geneva Motor Show, which testifies to the car's success and popularity. *(Author)*

↺ This young lady was pleased enough to have her photo taken alongside the new Ferrari California at the 2009 Geneva Motor Show. *(Author)*

The Pininfarina effect

Nowhere else in the history of the motor industry had one independent design house played such a pivotal role as that played by Pininfarina in the success of the styling of Ferrari's sports cars. Since 1952, Battista Farina, and later his son Sergio, have shaped and moulded Ferrari's position in the world of sports cars.

The success of Pininfarina's work at Ferrari and elsewhere in the industry earned him many awards and much recognition around the world.

In November 1983, Sergio Pininfarina was awarded the title of Honorary Royal Designer for Industry by the Royal Society of Arts, London. In 1991 he received the Designer Lifetime Achievement Award in Detroit for his contribution to the evolution of automotive style, granted for the first time to an Italian designer (one wonders why it had taken so long for this to be acknowledged).

On 30 March 1995 Pininfarina received the Career Award Compasso d'Oro for having demonstrated how to combine continuity and innovative aims and qualities in automobile design. Later that year he also received the first Design Award conferred by the respected motor journal *Auto Welt* for having exerted a unique influence on the evolution of automobile creativeness.

In 2002 the influential Royal College of Art conferred an Honorary Doctorate on Sergio Pininfarina at London's Royal Albert Hall in recognition of his great distinction both as a designer and as a design manager in over 50 years of activity. In 2007 Sergio was inducted into the Automotive Hall of Fame in Dearborn (Michigan), being considered 'among the great personalities who have profoundly affected the global motor vehicle industry', while a similar honour was bestowed on him when he was inducted into *Automotive News Europe*'s Automotive Hall of Fame in 2008.

The list of awards goes on, but the real proof of Battista and Sergio Pininfarina's contribution to the world of automotive design is surely confirmed by the fact that both father and son were consistently recognised over the years by the highest institutions in industry. On several occasions, honours were bestowed on Sergio many years after his father had received the same recognition. This is something unique in the history of the auto industry.

⊃ **In 2000, Pininfarina announced the Ferrari Rossa concept to celebrate the company's 70th anniversary.** *(Stefan Lüscher © Neill Bruce)*

Ferrari Rossa concept car (2000)

Sergio Pininfarina announced in 2000 that the Rossa concept car interpreted and advanced some of the key themes in the long-term partnership between Ferrari and Pininfarina, just as the Testa Rossa (1958) and the Mythos concept cars (1989) had done before.

Revealed at the Turin Motor Show in recognition of Pininfarina's 70 years in business, the Rossa research prototype received the Concept Car of the Year Award. Built on the Ferrari 550 Maranello chassis, the Rossa shared the same front-engine rear-drive layout.

The Rossa, which means red in Italian, was an attractive and spartan concept car with a purposeful and aggressive design. The front of the car features a rectangular central radiator grille flanked by a pair of large recessed brake ducts, while rather futuristic slit-like headlights reach back up the wings (fenders). In the centre of the bonnet the partially exposed 485bhp V12 engine is clearly visible.

Lateral flashes stretch back along either flank from the wheel-arches along the door caps and sills (rocker panels) emphasising the Rossa's speed, while the extremely low profile further highlights the car's streamlined and dramatic shape. Viewed from the side, the car's athletic stance reveals just how muscular and performance-orientated this concept was, with its extremely short rear overhang, while the sloping front section with relatively long front overhang gave the sports concept a very streamlined appearance.

The interior of the Rossa was functional and race-inspired, with racing bucket seats and four-point racing harnesses, but otherwise it was devoid of all comforts. Prominently located between driver and passenger was a large centre console which carried the traditional Ferrari H-gate gear-change selector. Each occupant was thus cocooned in their own space with only a low-angled windscreen to protect them from the inevitable wind rush.

⊃ **The driver was positioned well back in the Rossa concept, which featured the classic sports car proportions with its long bonnet and short tail.** *(Stefan Lüscher © Neill Bruce)*

↻ **The Rossa concept featured a no-frills interior. The exposed, or 'teardrop', rear lights, seen here, were first used on Ferrari's mid-engined cars in the early noughties, while the front-engined GT cars retained the recessed tail lights as in the original Daytona and the like.** *(Stefan Lüscher © Neill Bruce)*

↻ **This photo illustrates the wide and low stance of the 2000 Ferrari Rossa concept, which also featured many design elements that would appear on production cars soon afterwards.** *(Stefan Lüscher © Neill Bruce)*

The short and strong rear styling of the Rossa showed the teardrop tail lights which were seen on later production Ferraris, such as the Enzo and F430. With the popular and talented Japanese designer, Ken Okuyama, having penned both the Rossa and the Enzo while chief designer at Pininfarina, this development is perhaps unsurprising.

Enzo Ferrari (2002)

The day after clinching its fourth consecutive Formula 1 Constructor's Championship, Ferrari announced the arrival of its fastest-ever road car, the Enzo Ferrari. The company said it was 'the ultimate modern-day embodiment of the marque's passion for performance, technology, and dramatic style'.

The 220mph (350kph) supercar incorporated the company's latest advances from its Formula 1 adventures, including chassis, engine, and integrated electronic systems, enabling the driver to enjoy the car's extreme performance in safety. The Enzo was also a step back into history for the company to the days when Ferrari produced cars for the track that could be driven on the road too. The Enzo was the closest model yet to that early motor sport philosophy.

'Formula 1 has never offered our company such a genuine laboratory for advanced research as it has in recent years,' Ferrari President Luca di Montezemolo said in 2002. 'To combine our success on the track with the fundamental role of race car technology, I decided that this new car, as the pinnacle of our technological achievement, should be dedicated to our founder, who always felt that racing cars should lay the foundations of road car designs. So this model, of which we are all very proud, will be known as the Enzo Ferrari.'

As the natural successor to the F40 (1987) and F50 (1995), the extraordinary Enzo debuted at the 2002 Paris Motor Show. The Enzo was Maranello's supreme expression of the company's technology transfer from their Formula 1 programme to a GT road car. This limited-edition supercar was an aggressive, austere, no-compromise design, which in no uncertain terms consolidated Ferrari's position as the industry's leading manufacturer of extreme performance cars. According to Sergio Pininfarina, the Enzo was a pure, hard-line automobile with a strong character, which clearly reflected its Formula 1 links in the materials and technology used, and in its development and radical aerodynamics. Few could argue with that statement.

North American Ferrari aficionado, Mike Sheehan, put it this way: 'The new kid on the block is the Enzo, Ferrari's attempt to combine "Star Wars" styling with a real Formula 1 transmission that includes launch control.'

Dubbed 'di Montezemolo's F1 racer for the road', the Enzo's 5998cc, 660bhp V12 engine will rocket the car from 0–60mph in 3.6sec, and on to a top speed of 220mph (354kph).

The Enzo was the world's first car to be fitted with a fully-integrated electronic control system, and to use carbon ceramic brake discs, while other features derived from Formula 1 included ride-height-control technology, active aerodynamics, and built-in rear underbody diffusers. With World Formula 1 Champion Michael Schumacher on the panel of test drivers, the Enzo was always going to set the benchmark in this sector of the industry.

⊙ Not only did the Enzo break new boundaries in design, it also provided the factory with a platform for its new high-performance technology.
(Chr. Gonzenbach © Neill Bruce)

⊃ Ferrari's 2002 Enzo offered radical design thinking, taking the concept of aerodynamic efficiency to new levels.
(Chr. Gonzenbach © Neill Bruce)

● Parked in front of Wilton House, Wiltshire, home to William Herbert, 18th Earl of Pembroke, on the occasion of the Ferrari Owners Club annual picnic, this Enzo Ferrari seems at odds with its aristocratic background. However, it is this stark contrast that highlights the dramatic styling of the Enzo. *(Author)*

● Airflow management and cooling were important factors in the successful design and aerodynamic surfacing of the Enzo, making this vehicle a landmark design in the world of supercar engineering. *(Author)*

● So effective is the aerodynamic efficiency of the body that the Enzo requires no external aids to achieve downforce. *(Author)*

The Enzo's styling was the first Pininfarina-designed Ferrari to be so directly derived from its function. The car's nose section was heavily influenced by Formula 1 design, with the entire body being further shaped to ensure optimum airflow for cooling the engine and brakes, while generating unprecedented levels of downforce with minimal drag. In fact, the undercar ground-effects were so efficient that the large rear spoiler (wing) fitted to most other supercars was not required on the Enzo. At speed, the aerodynamic balance of the Enzo was maintained by

automatic adjustments to the position of twin front flaps and a single rear spoiler.

Weighing just 202lb (90kg), the chassis was fabricated from aluminium honeycomb sandwich panels, while the body was made using advanced composite materials. Access to the cabin is through scissor doors that hinge upwards.

Overall styling is characterised by the large front air scoops and the side-mounted intakes located aft of the doors. Quad exhausts are divided into two double outlets each side, from which emanates a V12 symphony, courtesy of the six-litre 660bhp engine, which lets other road users know what has just passed them. Dual round teardrop-shaped light clusters 'pop out' of the trailing edge of the engine cover, highlighting the extremely wide back-end dimensions (2,035mm/80in, compared with the 360 Modena's 1,922mm/76in width).

Only 349 Enzos (all left-hand-drive) were made by Ferrari, and at a price of £425,000 they were destined for just a lucky few.

612 Scaglietti (2004)

Announced to the press in October 2003, the new 612 Scaglietti debuted at the Detroit Motor Show in January the following year. Ferrari's new 2+2 replaced the earlier 456 GT and 456M GT models, which had been in production since 1993 (3,260 of this model were produced between 1993 and 2003).

In the 612, Pininfarina sought to provide the Berlinetta's occupants with even more comfort and luxury as they were whisked along by the potent 5748cc V12 front-mid-mounted engine. Named after the well-known Ferrari coachbuilder, Sergio Scaglietti, the new 612 was a substantial 4,902mm (193in) in length, 172mm (nearly 7in) longer than its predecessor. In order to illustrate the lengths (no pun intended) to which Pininfarina went to achieve a better ride, the wheelbase of the 612, at 2,950mm (116in), is a good 350mm (nearly 14in) longer than the 456 model.

Pininfarina claimed that the 612 Scaglietti was the 'perfect marriage' of sporty thoroughbred Ferrari Berlinetta performance and excellent onboard comfort. As the third new model of the millennium (if one counts the 360 Modena of 1999), the 612 Scaglietti offered a whole new generation of technologies compared to the 2+2 it replaced. In keeping with a tradition that was started by the 250 GT 2+2 (launched at the Paris Motor Show in 1960), the 612 was a genuine, roomier two-door four-seater (at 1,344mm/53in, it was 44mm/nearly 2in higher than the 456 model) that offered its occupants an altogether more comfortable and pleasant ride. The car's modern styling was aggressive yet eye-catchingly elegant, and to ensure that the occupants could really go travelling in style, the coupé offered 25 per cent more luggage space than its predecessor.

Designed by Pininfarina, but made entirely at the Scaglietti works in Maranello, the 612 was the first 12-cylinder Ferrari to be made entirely from aluminium. This resulted in a 60 per cent more rigid construction and a weight saving of 132lb (60kg).

⊃⌒ The Ferrari 612 Scaglietti undergoes a road test by Swiss auto journal *Auto Illustrierte*, on the occasion of the car's European press launch in 2004. *(R. Meinert © Neill Bruce)*

Following the bottom edge of the front radiator grille, a distinctive dihedral line could be traced backwards on either side up through the headlamps and along the wing (fender) tops and doors to the rear shoulders. This left the rear volume with a more rounded and muscular shape, which was finished with Ferrari's traditional twin round light clusters, successfully combining tradition with innovation.

Large scalloped features on either side were reminiscent of the 1954 Pininfarina-bodied 375 MM Paris show car given to Ingrid Bergman by her Italian film director husband, Roberto Rossellini. Pininfarina designer Ken Okuyama can be credited with recreating this link

⊃ The author (right) was given a blast up the hill in this Ferrari 612 Scaglietti at the 2008 Goodwood Festival of Speed. This car was one of the two similarly prepared 612s that had just successfully completed the Ferrari tour of the Indian sub-continent. The following day it was to be shipped to its permanent home in the Ferrari Museum in Maranello, making the author one of the last lucky few to have been driven in this vehicle – and with some vigour, I might add! *(Author)*

⊃ One could expect applications for new recruits in the Italian Police Department to increase suddenly and dramatically if they were given cars such as the 612 Scaglietti in which to patrol the streets. *(Author)*

with Ferrari's past, and in so doing he introduced a strong element of grace in this modern businessman's express.

Introduced in 2004, the 612 Scaglietti could be fitted with Ferrari's special HGT-S (Handling-GTS) pack. Cosmetically, the changes are limited to 19in wheels at the front and yellow brake callipers, but under the skin this option included sports exhausts with valves that open at 3,000rpm (making the V12 symphony even more pleasant), a revised control system for the adaptive suspension, and shorter gear change times. The HGT-S option also included the F1A electro-hydraulic transmission with revised software for faster gear changes.

grown up into a strapping, mature, and very desirable athlete. *Top Gear* magazine voted the F430 'Supercar of the year' in December of that year.

The 'F' prefix was back, having skipped the 360, but one was left in no doubt as to 430's origins, as the gap between these two was not as great as between the 360 Modena and its predecessor, the F355. Front-end styling on the newcomer featured significantly larger radiator air intakes located on either side of the bumper, with a slender headlamp grouping that reached backwards 'up' the wing (fender). The lower forward lateral radiator exits ahead of the front wheels were also significantly larger and vertically orientated, allowing air to pass more easily through the tall slits. Located between the front radiator intakes was a small, horizontal element (similar to that of the Enzo), which directed air under the car's flat underbody, speeding up and smoothing the flow of air through to the rear diffuser.

Stretching along the sills (rocker panels) between the wheel-arches, the F430's air duct was revised and slightly more pronounced than its predecessor, while the shoulder-mounted engine intakes were larger, protruding upwards in a more purposeful fashion than on the 360. The larger nose intakes and the more pronounced upper air intakes just aft of the doors both harked back to racing models of the 1960s, the former resembling the 'Sharknose' 156 Formula 1 of 1961, while the 1963 250 LM sports racer inspired the upper air intakes mounted on the shoulders.

Compared with its predecessor, the 430's back-end view (which most other motorists would get to see) showed some modernisation and revision. Although the newer model would share the same transparent engine cover, this was now flanked on either side by a narrow strip of air vents, while immediately below the trailing edge of the engine cover was a mesh air intake which carried a floating 'Prancing Horse'. The tail carried a discreet but raised lip which worked with the more prominent underbody diffuser to ensure a smooth flow of air off the body, while the rear bumper was more cleanly integrated into the rear body than on the 360. Although both the 360 and 430 featured twin round rear light groupings, the later car had its light pairings high-mounted as in the Enzo, in what was called the 'teardrop' shape.

Pininfarina's body design was driven by the F430's advanced technical content and set-up. All body design features on the F430 emphasise the car's aggressive

○ Ferrari's F430 lifted the bar in the junior supercar stakes, not just on the performance, quality, and comfort fronts, but also in terms of style – the F430 was one mature sports car. *(LAT)*

Ferrari F430 (2004)

There comes a point in every young man's life when, all of a sudden, he becomes grown up, and though it may be difficult to pin down the transformation to a single day or event, he nevertheless knows that it has happened. In the same way, when Ferrari unveiled the F430 at the 2004 Paris Motor Show there was no mistaking that Ferrari's compact mid-engined junior sports car had

Ferrari 360 Modena and F430 body dimensions comparison

Dimension	360 Modena (1999)	F430 (2004)
Wheelbase (mm)	2,600	2,600
Track front/rear (mm)	1,669/1,617	1,669/1,617
Length (mm)	4,477	4,512
Width (mm)	1,922	1,923
Height (mm)	1,235	1,214
Kerb weight (kg)	1,350	1,350

Source: Ferrari press kits

⊃ **Developing 490bhp, the F430's 4.3-litre V8 engine produced 90bhp more than its older 360 sibling (400bhp). The sports car's sophisticated underbody culminated in a comprehensively redesigned rear diffuser.** *(LAT)*

ↀ **Ferrari's F430 can trace its V8 mid-engined heritage back to the 1973 Bertone Dino 308 GT/4, or one could even go as far as the Dino 206 GT if you include its V6 forefather.** *(Author)*

ↀ **The F430's superb overbody airflow meant that no exterior aerodynamic aids were required to ensure downforce and stability at speed. This was instead achieved through efficient underbody airflow management combined with a discreet boot lip and rear deck airflow.** *(Author)*

style and performance, and were in response to precise functional requirements as regards engine cooling flows and fuel feed aerodynamic properties, as well as the sophisticated shape of the floorpan and rear diffuser with vertical fins (again, similar to those found on the Enzo) which ensured adequate negative lift.

Fitted with a substantially increased capacity engine (the F430 engine was an all-new unit and did not share any components with the 360's engine), this 4308cc punched out 490bhp and enabled the sports car to reach a top speed of 196mph (315kph) and could cover the 0–62mph (0–100kph) sprint in just 4sec. The F430 is the first V8 Ferrari to feature driver-aid controls on the

Ferrari F430 Spider at the Eau Rouge curves at the foot of the awesome downhill section of the Spa Francorchamps old pit straight. Even in this soft-top Ferrari, the concave rear window is reminiscent of the first road-going mid-engined sports car to come from Maranello, the Dino 206. *(Author)*

Attractive from any angle, the F430 Spider cuts a striking pose displaying immense presence and grace for a convertible sports car. *(Author)*

⊃ True to Ferrari tradition, the Ferrari's F430 Spider engine is visible through the transparent engine cover. *(Author)*

⌒ The Ferrari F430 Spider at the bottom of the famous Eau Rouge corner on the Spa Francorchamps circuit in August 2008, where just an hour earlier race cars had done battle at dizzying speeds. The Grigio Alloy (silver/grey) Spider soft-top contrasts strikingly with the heavy storm clouds in the background following an eventful 24-hour race at the famous Belgian circuit. *(Author)*

steering wheel, as seen previously on the Enzo and 612 Scaglietti, and known to Ferrari Formula 1 drivers as the 'manettino' – a switch on the lower right sector of the steering wheel that controls the car's dynamic set-up modes according to road conditions (Ice, Low Grip, Sport, and Race).

Debuting at the 2005 Geneva Motor Show was the open version of the F430, the Spider, marking 75 years of activity by Pininfarina. Mounted behind each seat was a streamlined hump which hid the dual roll-over bars, but the absence of a solid roof in no way affected the smooth lines of the Spider, as is commonly found in many soft top derivatives when compared with their respective coupé siblings. Thanks to the attractively low windscreen line of the Spider, this car is every bit as assertive and purposeful as its stablemate.

As a result of an engineering approach similar to that employed in the development of their Formula 1 cars, Ferrari created a highly efficient aerodynamic package that channelled airflow for optimum downforce as well as engine performance. This attention to efficiency resulted in an increase in downforce of 40 per cent when compared with the 360 Spider. Air diverted around and under the car, thanks to the development of a new spoiler, resulted in an impressive 125kg (275lb) of downforce on the front axle, greatly increasing stability. Similarly,

vertical fences (deflectors) in the rear underbody diffuser work in conjunction with the tail spoiler to speed up the airflow over the rear of the body, adding 135kg (298lb) of downforce at the rear for a total of 260kg (573lb) at a speed of 186mph (300kph).

The folding roof is driven by as many as 14 motors and folds into a section between the engine and the passenger compartment. A weight penalty of 152lb (70kg), because of the additional chassis strengthening, knocks a few miles per hour off the top end, but this is still one seriously fast and very beautiful open-top sports car.

A Ferrari F430 Spider featured in the 2006 American movie, *Miami Vice*, in which two detectives worked undercover investigating a narcotics-smuggling operation in Florida. Featuring a genuine Grigio Silverstone (grey to most folk) Spider, instead of the fake Daytonas used in the original television series, Ferrari were no doubt hoping to recapture some of the *Magnum P.I.* detective magic from the 1980s in which the 308 GTS was used so successfully.

The Frankfurt Motor Show (11 September 2007) was selected as the venue for the unveiling of a new Ferrari model, the 430 Scuderia. This special series model was based on the F430 and, being developed specifically with Ferrari's sportiest clients in mind, this new extremely high performance two-seater Berlinetta was brimming with Formula 1-derived technology.

The 430 Scuderia was officially unveiled at the show by Michael Schumacher, who contributed to its development at different stages, further strengthening the link between this new model and Ferrari's Formula 1 single-seaters. Lightweight and simple, every last detail of the Ferrari 430 Scuderia, in character with its name, boasted uncompromising sportiness.

The car's aerodynamic efficiency was enhanced by a new-style rear diffuser, combined with a revised-profile spoiler at the rear of the engine cover, while the addition of large venturis, running from the front wheel-arches to the rear bumpers, achieved the patented Base Bleed effect. (Developed by Ferrari as part of their FXX project, Base Bleed reduces air pressure in the rear wheel-arches, thereby increasing downforce and lowering drag.) The new lower sill profiles provided a more uniform distribution of airflow over the lower parts, ensuring uniform distribution of the vertical load between the front and the rear of the car.

➲ The badge says it all – Ferrari's awesome F430 Scuderia was launched at the Frankfurt Motor Show in 2007. *(Author)*

⏻ On the turntable, Ferrari's F430 Scuderia takes centre stage at Frankfurt in 2007. *(Author)*

⋒ It is difficult not to have people in the frame when photographing a Ferrari – the F430 Scuderia was a magnet at the 2008 Geneva Motor Show. The revised air duct just ahead of the front wheels permits smoother airflow. *(Author)*

⊂ From this low angle one can get a good idea of the aerodynamic work done on the front intake ducts of the Ferrari F430. *(Author)*

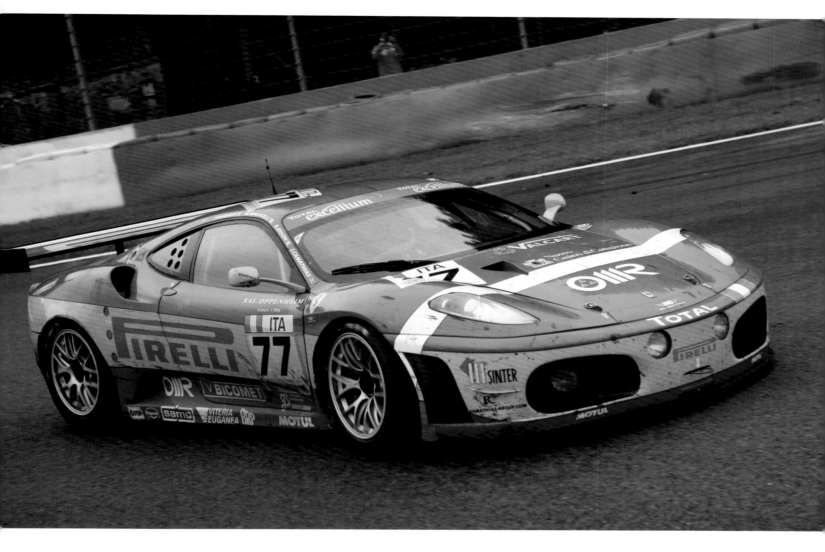

Carbon-fibre was extensively used in an effort to reduce the car's weight (220lb/100kg was shed), and customers could order special carbon-fibre kits, which included the front spoiler, headlamp assembly, sills, engine cover, and diffuser. For the really serious driver, a carbon-fibre helmet was also produced.

With a dry weight of just 1,250kg (2,755lb) and 510bhp, delivered at 8,500rpm by its naturally-aspirated 4308cc V8 engine, the 430 Scuderia can sprint from 0–62mph (0–100kph) in just 3.6 seconds.

The Scuderia is to the F430 what the Porsche GT3 is to the standard 911, or perhaps what the Lamborghini Superleggera is to the Gallardo. You get the same impressive looks, but the adrenalin rush from driving the car is indescribable. It's like trying to explain how it is when the hair stands up on the back of your neck – words are just not enough.

Developed in conjunction with Michelotti, the F430 GT was an even more stripped down version of the roadgoing Scuderia, and is aimed purely at endurance racing. The F430 GT's major race debut was at the 12 Hours of Sebring in 2006 where the Risi Competizione Ferrari finished 11th overall, and third in the GT2 class, an impressive result for this 'out of the box' racer. The F430 GT boasted a new body comprising a combination of carbon-fibre, Nomex, and Kevlar, which resulted in a weight of just 1,100kg (2,425lb).

The F430 GT went on to trounce the Porsche 911 GT3 RSRs at Le Mans in 2009, taking nine of the first ten places in the GT2 class. The only Porsche to finish was in a distant 12th place.

The Porsche company is well known for creating commemorative models to mark anniversaries and important occasions, with favourable financial results,

Although, for many years, Ferrari had not competed with a factory team in the GT classes, numerous client teams had done so around the world. The No. 77 BMS Scuderia Italia Ferrari F430 GT, photographed here, finished 5th overall and first in the GT2 class in the 2008 Spa 24 Hours. Here, the car rounds the La Source hairpin, just before entering the old start/finish straight past the pits. (Author)

⌒ This Ferrari Scuderia
Spider 16M, in Grigio
Titanio livery, was shown
at the 79th Geneva Motor
Show in March 2009.

(Author)

⌒ Ferrari's Scuderia
Spider 16M is a lightened
version of the F430 Spider.

(Author)

and it appears that Ferrari jumped on the same lucrative bandwagon in creating the Scuderia Spider 16M. This very special, high-performance model, created to commemorate Ferrari's 16th Formula 1 Constructors title, debuted at the Ferrari World Finals in Mugello on 9 November 2008. The World Finals, traditionally the closing event of the motor sport season, was a fitting venue at which to launch the 16M, which at 2,954lb/1,340kg was 176lb/80kg lighter than the F430 Spider, along with a modified version of the F430 Spider.

Limited to just 499 examples worldwide, the Scuderia Spider 16M featured the same high-performance handling as the 430 Scuderia, but included some additional livery options and interior detailing.

Punching out the same 510bhp as the Scuderia Berlinetta, the Spider 16M could accelerate from standstill to 62mph (100kph) in just 3.7sec, and go on to a top speed of 198mph (315kph). The 16M was reported by the factory as Ferrari's fastest convertible car around the company's Fiorano test track in Maranello.

◠ **A revised, performance-enhancing rear diffuser is just part of the new aero package on this new Ferrari Scuderia Spider 16M.** *(Author)*

Ferrari Superamerica (2005)

Today the concept of a coupé convertible has become a marketing niche in its own right, but the Pininfarina-designed Superamerica was certainly one of the first to combine the characteristics of a Berlinetta with the concept of a convertible. But, this was no conventional folding roof. Rather, it was a state-of-the-art glass top that rotated within the confines of the rear uprights or B-pillars.

Announced on 24 November 2004, the Ferrari Superamerica was a limited edition model, which premiered at the Los Angeles and Detroit Motor Shows in January the following year. The name Superamerica, traditionally only associated with Ferrari's prestigious and limited production cars, was derived from the 575M Maranello. While the front-end styling is familiar, the cabin and rear section of the car are unique.

One of the drawbacks of having a folding solid roof is that it has to be stored somewhere, and today this is usually cleverly retracted into the conventional rear boot, leaving little or no space for luggage. However, the Superamerica's innovative roof remains rigid, rotating upwards and rearwards about swivel points mounted on the inside of the rear buttresses, leaving the boot capacity unchanged irrespective of whether the roof is open or closed. When in the open position, the solid rear window is simply inverted, providing a convenient windshield for the occupants.

↻ The name 'Superamerica' invokes memories of Ferrari's 1950s super-styled sports cars. This styling is almost 'boxy' by comparison, but today's sports cars have to carry so much more by way of technology. *(LAT)*

↻ The Ferrari Superamerica drew huge crowds at the Goodwood Festival of Speed in 2006. This close-up shows the swivel mechanism for the innovative roof. *(Author)*

⊂ The Ferrari Superamerica was made for days like this – sunshine and picnics. *(Author)*

⊂ The Superamerica's roof structure and rear body design make an interesting study – one could almost compare the flying buttresses of this car to the controversial styling of Porsche's Panamericana concept of 1989 where the top line of the windscreen is swept backwards to finish at the tail. *(Author)*

Ferrari 575M Maranello and Superamerica body dimensions compared

Dimension	575M Maranello (2002)	Superamerica (2005)
Wheelbase (mm)	2,500	2,500
Track front/rear (mm)	1,632/1,586	1,632/1,586
Length (mm)	4,555	4,550
Width (mm)	1,935	1,935
Height (mm)	1,277	1,277
Kerb weight (kg)	1,730	1,790

Source: Ferrari press kits

This exclusive Fioravanti-designed electric rotating roof movement allows the driver to convert the Superamerica from a sports coupé into a fully-convertible sports car in just ten seconds. Dubbed the 'Revocromico', the roof is also far from being just a clever rotating system, as the top glass component employed electrochromic technology developed with French glass manufacturers, Saint Gobain. Held firmly in a carbon-fibre structure, the use of electrochromic glass meant that, with the roof closed, the driver could control the level of light entering the cockpit by a choice of five tint levels which went from dark to light in under a minute at the touch of a button.

The Superamerica features a 5748cc V12 engine, and its 540bhp was sufficient to propel the car to a top speed of 200mph (320kph). This sort of performance made it the world's fastest convertible Berlinetta at the time, in keeping with the Ferrari tradition for its Superamerica name.

Ferrari 599 GTB Fiorano (2006)

At the Detroit Motor Show on 9 January 2006, Amedeo Felisa, Ferrari's Vice General Manager, announced the imminent arrival of Ferrari's latest front-engined V12 grand tourer, a new GTB or Gran Turismo Berlinetta. The newcomer's public debut, however, would be reserved for the Geneva Motor Show on 28 February of that year, where it appeared on the Pininfarina stand.

The late Andrea Pininfarina recalled that when handing over the briefing document for its new mid-front-engined two-seater coupé, Ferrari President Luca Cordero di Montezemolo specified that, in terms of sportiness, performance, exciting driving, and aggressive styling, the car was to conjure up the same emotions as those aroused by the F40 supercar when it was presented in 1987.

Replacing the 575M Maranello (which together with the 550 Maranello introduced in 1996 had resulted in the sale of 5,700 units), the 599 GTB Fiorano slotted neatly between the 'entry level' F430 and the flagship 612 Scaglietti. The 599 was set to continue in the true Ferrari Berlinetta tradition which could trace its bloodline back to the 250 MM (1953), and which continued through such icons as the 250 GT (1959), 275 GTB (1964), 365 GTB4 (1968), and 575M Maranello (2002) models.

While dimensionally smaller than the 612, the 599's V12 engine displaced 6 litres against the 5.75 litres of the 612. Producing 620bhp (the 612 was good for 532bhp), the 599 GTB Fiorano was certainly Ferrari's most powerful road-going sports car, and probably one of the most powerful in the world at that time.

Not for nothing was this model named Fiorano, after the company's own race track, where most of its road development was carried out. Its all-aluminium space frame was developed in partnership with Alcoa, and its mid-front located 5999cc V12 engine was derived directly from the Enzo Ferrari mid-engined supercar.

⌒ **Making its UK debut at the Goodwood Festival of Speed in 2007 was this 599 GTB Fiorano.** *(Author)*

The lightness of frame, which delivered a 50 per cent improvement in torsional rigidity/weight over the 575M Maranello, combined with the astonishingly powerful engine, ensured a blisteringly quick acceleration time for the 0–62mph (0–100kph) sprint of just 3.7sec.

The 599's design was developed around front-sloping lines, which gave the car a dynamic stance when viewed from the side. The front wings (fenders) extended forward into the front bumpers so that it seemed that the central section, comprising the bonnet and central vent, was set into them. The front section was strikingly sculptured with one of the main visual features being the prominent power bulge in the bonnet.

With the engine and fuel tank located between the axles and the cabin pulled back, an optimal weight distribution of 47 per cent front and 53 per cent rear was achieved. With these improvements, the engineers were able to lower the car's centre of gravity by 20mm (¾in) compared to the 575M Maranello.

The Pininfarina-designed body featured aggressive yet elegant lines that incorporated advanced functional aerodynamic elements such as the cooling and intake vents which were integrated into the design of the body. Up front, the classic central Ferrari vent optimised the flow of air towards the radiator, while two inlets, which flanked the central intake, supplied cooling air to the brakes and the intake ducts of the engine.

Dihedral lines which started in the centre of the front headlamps continued back along the wings (fenders), and could be traced along the door tops to the trailing edge of the rear wings (fenders), finishing just above the rear lights. This feature encouraged the eye to see the design of the 599 GTB Fiorano as one continuous form, giving the sports car a fresh and modern appearance.

The side view is a fine example of a modern interpretation of the true Ferrari GTB concept, featuring slightly sharper styling, while still retaining the shapely curves of yesteryear. The long, muscular bonnet, leaving you in no doubt as to the location of the engine, was in contrast to the short but attractive tail. In accordance with the tradition set by the Ferrari Berlinettas of years gone by, the 599 continued the styling with round rear light clusters, but now featuring Ferrari's trademark exposed upper surfaces. Lateral hot air exit vents, positioned just behind the front wheel-arches and quite high up on the wings (fenders), featured stylish flashes which reached back along the flanks of the doors, while the correspondingly low-level cooling ducts for the fuel tank and gearbox mimicked this rakish style. These features contributed to the muscular surfacing of the car's flanks.

The 599's high rear haunches highlighted the car's muscular, forceful look, while still successfully presenting a strikingly simple shape. According to Fabrizio Valentini, Pininfarina Design Vice Director, the 599's innovative rear roof pillars did not merely have a static function, but were detached from the surface of the characteristic Berlinetta teardrop rear window and acted as aerodynamic 'flying buttresses', contributing towards the vehicle's negative lift and stability.

A small nolder on the trailing edge of the boot contributed to the car's aerodynamic efficiency, increasing downforce and resulting in a lift factor (Cz) of 0.190 and a Cd of 0.336.

At the 79th Geneva International Motor Show on 3 March 2009, Ferrari introduced its Handling GT Evoluzione (HGTE) package for the 599 GTB Fiorano. Although the outward appearance of the car changed very little, the technical modifications introduced with the HGTE package ensured more dynamic handling with improved responsiveness, whilst still remaining an easy car to drive. From a styling point of view, external modifications included 20in split-rim wheels (which saved 11lb/5kg in unsprung weight) and the rear diffuser was finished in matt black.

⋂ **Innovative detached flying buttresses enhanced the aerodynamic efficiency of the 599 GTB Fiorano.** (Author)

⌒ **Ferrari first used large single round tail lights as far back as the 1962 250 GTL Lusso, but it was probably the 275 GTB of 1964 which established the style for Ferrari. The 599 GTB continued this design tradition.** (Author)

It must rank as one of the fastest safety cars in the business – this Ferrari 599 GTB Fiorano was employed as the Silverstone Safety Car at Ferrari's 60th anniversary celebrations at the Northampton circuit in June 2007. *(Author)*

SAFETY CAR

V12 SFT

Ferrari launched the HGTE at the 2009 Geneva Motor Show, an expensive handling option for 599 GTB Fiorano owners. *(Author)*

The 2009 Geneva Motor Show was also witness to the world debut of the 599XX, an all-out track car aimed at a select group of owners who wanted to enjoy genuine race action without having to commit to the requirements of a full race season. For those customers, Ferrari would organise a programme of dedicated track events in 2010/2011. Conceived exclusively for the track but not for official competition use, the 599XX benefited from unrestricted homologation limitations, thus allowing Ferrari the freedom to experiment with and develop race car features without risking actual championship positions. Reflections of the 275 GT Competizione (1956) can be seen in the thinking behind this model.

⌒ For those wanting to personalise their 599 even further, the German specialist customisation firm, Mansory, offered this Ferrari 599 GTB Fiorano Stallone at the 2008 Geneva Motor Show. *(Author)*

⌒ The Ferrari 599XX shown at the 2009 Geneva Motor Show. The plethora of aerodynamic, electronic control, and handling innovations, used together for the first time on a single car, make this model a genuine technical laboratory. *(Author)*

Ferrari's engineers carried out extensive engine developments, which helped achieve the target power output of 700bhp. The 599XX's aerodynamics were honed in numerous windtunnel test sessions, with the result that the car boasted more than 600lb (280kg) of downforce at 125mph (200kph) and almost 1,400lb (630kg) at 190mph (300kph). The front underside of the body was completely faired-in, and the vents that channeled hot air from the engine bay were moved to the bonnet.

Ferrari's 'Actiflow' system increased downforce and/or cut drag depending on the car's trim, courtesy of the use of a porous material in the diffuser, while two fans in the boot channelled the airflow, from under the car, out through the tail lights. Synthetic jets were also incorporated into the rear of the car to control and smooth the airflow and to reduce drag. Ferrari's engineers also fitted Formula 1-derived 'doughnuts' that partly covered the brake discs and wheel rim. These had the dual function of improving both aerodynamics and brake cooling. In terms of the bodywork, composites and carbon-fibre were widely used.

ⓐ Underbody air is funnelled out through the rear light apertures, while the 599XX features a full race underbody diffuser. *(Author)*

ⓑ Note the side winglet mounted high on the rear roof pillar of the Ferrari 599XX, as well as the vertical blades just aft of the rear wheels, which also mirror those just behind the front wheels. *(Author)*

⊂∪ This magnificent Ferrari 250 GT California Spyder No. 2377, belonging to radio DJ Chris Evans, was seen at the 2008 Goodwood Festival of Speed. Once the property of actor James Coburn, this model is widely regarded as one of the most beautiful of Pininfarina's creations.

(Author)

Ferrari California (2008)

Back in the 1950s and 1960s when Ferrari aroused the emotional buying power of the American public with models such as the America, Mexico, Superamerica, Superfast, California, and Daytona, these names really meant something to motor sport enthusiasts. Several of these models were named after particularly successful racing campaigns, while others were intended to appeal to a more affluent market where luxury and style were the order of the day.

One of these models, the 250 GT California Spyder, built in two series between 1957–60 and 1960–3, was so named to appeal to American West Coast customers, amongst whom Hollywood film stars were the company's regular clientele. Today, these cars are among the most desirable Ferraris in collectors' circles.

Launched in 2008, and bristling with up-to-date features and new technologies, the new California was the first Ferrari designed specifically to attract women to the brand. There are plenty of women who appreciate

↻ Shown at the 2009 Geneva Motor Show was this Ferrari California finished in Nero Metallizzato with a Sabbia interior. *(Author)*

↻ Perhaps the styling feature that the California is remembered for more than any other is the controversial 'swish' along its flanks. *(Author)*

drivers' cars, and Ferrari was hoping that 50 per cent of California buyers would be of the fairer sex.

Ferrari broke new ground on several fronts with the introduction of the California, as the premiere, which took place in Maranello on 18 September 2008, was viewed simultaneously in Los Angeles and around the world by registered Ferrari enthusiasts on a dedicated California website. This was followed a fortnight later (on 2 October) by the official public unveiling at the Paris Motor Show.

In typical flamboyant style, Ferrari President Luca di Montezemolo made the announcement in Maranello, ably supported by his Formula 1 drivers Kimi Räikkönen and Felipe Massa. Also to hand was seven times world champion Michael Schumacher, who from the beginning had been deeply involved with the development of the California. Attending the Los Angeles event was the Governor of California, Arnold Schwarzenegger, which is a little ironic since he heads the administration that bangs the greenest drum in the USA.

As mentioned above, this new sports car represented several firsts for Ferrari, one being the front-mid-mounted direct-injection 4.3-litre V8 engine, producing 460bhp. Another was that this 2+2 convertible coupé was fitted with a folding hard top that could be opened or closed in just 14sec, and which retracted into the boot (which explains the car's high waistline and relatively chunky rear).

However, chunky or not, the California's proportions are remarkably smooth for what the car had to offer. The high boot line is balanced by the height of the bonnet, which slopes quite dramatically towards the front bumper, disguising the car's height rather well. The accompanying table shows the comparative body dimensions of the California and Ferrari's previous open-top model, the 550 Barchetta, and makes for interesting reading.

It can be seen that while the 550 Barchetta was shorter, it was also wider and lower, the additional height in the body of the California being necessary to accommodate the folded roof in the boot when down, while still

Comparison of body dimensions for the 550 Barchetta and California

Dimension (mm)	550 Barchetta (2000)	California (2008)
Length	4,550	4,563
Width	1,935	1,902
Height	1,258	1,308
Wheelbase	2,500	2,670
Front track	1,632	1,630
Rear track	1,586	1,605

Source: Ferrari press kits

providing sufficient storage space for weekends away. In fact, with the roof raised, the boot's total capacity is 340l (12cu ft), and when retracted and folded into the boot there is still an impressive 240l (8½cu ft) of available capacity, ideal for those essential shopping trips to Sachs, Gucci, and the like.

But those who thought that a Ferrari designed to appeal to the fairer sex would result in a softer car (disconnected from its sports car heritage) were right off the mark. As Ferrari said in its promotional literature, the California is a car with 'one heart and two souls'. The 'one heart' refers to the thoroughbred engine, Ferrari's hallmark of performance, while the 'two souls' allude to the option of coupé-style touring or open-top cruising.

⋂ **This close-up three-quarter angle shows the bulk of the California's back end, with the boot lid almost the same height as the top of the headrests.** *(Author)*

⊃ **The California's 'swish', which originates at the engine exit vent on the front wing (fender) and travels the full length of the body, terminating at the rear light.** *(Author)*

↻ **What owning a California is all about – enjoying a day out in the sunshine – and Ferrari will be pleased to know that in this photo at least they have achieved their marketing aspirations since, of the two people shown, the lady is the owner. The author is not sure, though, that the car's registration is appropriate for a sports car like the California.** *(Author)*

Some commentators, including one leading motor journal, have criticised the California's lateral 'scoops', which start behind the exit vents in the front wing (fender) and run the full length of the car to the rear lights. Dale Harrow had this to say: 'Those scoops down the side … it is very hard to put them there and say that they improve the car's efficiency. It looks like a bit of bad styling, but I am sure that the car will do very well in the States.'

The design of the California was by Pininfarina once again, but this time they worked in collaboration with Ferrari's in-house Styling Centre. Like it or loathe it, the car's lateral styling, with its strong flowing lines rising above the door handles, gives a muscular outline to its rear wings. Much work was done on the California's

⋂ The California's twin vertically-stacked tailpipes are a novel styling feature on this newcomer. *(Author)*

⊂ The Ferrari California was also a feature on the Pininfarina stand at the 2009 Geneva Motor Show. Several design renderings can be seen on the panels in the background. *(Author)*

The Ferrari California is put through its paces during its UK debut at the 2009 Goodwood Festival of Speed. It is interesting to note how the designers have created styling 'scallops', which start at the base of the windscreen and sweep around the base of the headlamps. This serves to further enhance the muscular styling of the bonnet with its central power bulge and air scoop, reminiscent of the 1957 California 250. *(Author)*

aerodynamic styling, which, in coupé configuration, resulted in a drag coefficient of 0.32.

The California's rear end is an impressive combination of styling and function. Underscoring the car's ample output is the quad exhaust system, comprising two pairs of vertically-stacked tailpipes, one pair each side of the body. The teardrop tail lights are a recent Ferrari styling trademark, and in this case they pierce the curvaceous boot surface. A discreet boot lip acts in conjunction with the underbody diffuser to improve the overbody airflow and aerodynamics.

458 Italia (2009)

Launched on 15 September 2009 at the 63rd IAA Frankfurt Motor Show, the new 458 Italia showcased Ferrari's latest mechanical and aerodynamic technology. Replacing the F430, this newcomer featured an increased engine capacity (4499cc) and represented quite a surprising visual departure from the mid-engined lineage that preceded this model.

This two-seater Berlinetta follows the traditional Ferrari mid-rear-engine layout, but despite an even larger engine, advances in aerodynamics enabled the design engineers to relocate many of the air intake ducts, giving the 458 an altogether much cleaner appearance. The Pininfarina-designed shape is a combination of modern, sharp surfaces and the traditional sweeping flanks seen on previous mid-engined Ferraris.

The nose section features a single opening (as opposed to the triple opening of the F430) for the front grille and side air intakes, with aerodynamic sections and profiles designed to direct air to the coolant radiators and the new flat underbody. The nose also sports small aeroelastic winglets, which generate downforce and, as the car's speed rises, deform to reduce the section of the radiator intake and cut drag. The trapezoidal-shaped coolant radiators are positioned to minimise the impact of the internal cooling flows on drag and downforce.

The oil radiators for the gearbox and dual-clutch are situated in the tail, and air is fed to them through two intakes located on the top of the rear wings. This provides a Base Bleed effect, an aerodynamic function

⋒ The Ferrari stand at the IAA Frankfurt Motor Show on 15 September 2009 featured a pair of the company's new 458 Italia mid-engined sports cars. Nearest the camera is the Rosso Corsa (red) model, while the Giallo Modena Tristrato (yellow) example is on the far side. *(Author)*

⋐ Now used on all Ferrari road-going sports cars, including the new 458 Italia, is the hallmark round rear light first seen in the early 1960s. *(Author)*

⋔ **Neatly recessed vents on the upper rear bodywork of the 458 Italia direct cooling air to the gearbox and oil radiators.** *(Author)*

⊃ **The three tailpipe combination at the back of the 458 Italia is a work of art in itself, requiring the siamesing of exhaust pipes to result in this ingenious threesome.** *(Author)*

⊃ **Different front-end styling treatment on the 458 Italia distinguishes it from the F430 front which featured a central panel in body colour. This wide grin gives the new car a distinctive look.** *(Author)*

that was developed for the FXX and which reduces drag by feeding the hot air out of the radiators under the nolder and into the car's low-pressure slipstream. Air intakes for engine bay cooling (similar to those on the F430 GT2) are located in the car's aerodynamic underbody ahead of the rear wheel-arches where they use pressure differences to channel airflow to the engine bay, at the same time generating more rear downforce. This development has eliminated the need for lateral air intake ducts traditionally located on the car's shoulder or at sill (rocker panel) level.

By relocating the low level air intakes, the engineers have added two keel forms that act as fairings to the rear wheels. The bodywork between the rear diffusers accommodates the triple exhaust tailpipes, an F40 styling cue that gives the 458 Italia's tail an aggressive sporty appearance, while the engine is visible through the transparent engine cover, just like the F430 and 360 Modena before it.

Computational Fluid Dynamic (CFD) techniques helped optimise the management and interaction of the internal flows prior to modular 1:3 scale model wind tunnel testing. This enabled the engineers to achieve excellent drag and downforce figures (Cd 0.33 and Cl 0.36 respectively) with 140kg (309lb) of downforce at 200kph (124mph) and no less than 360kg (794lb) at top speed. This high level of aerodynamic efficiency

Ferrari F430 and 458 Italia body dimensions comparison:

Dimension	F430 (2004)	458 Italia (2009)
Wheelbase (mm)	2,600	2,650
Track front/rear (mm)	1,669/1,617	1,672/1,606
Length (mm)	4,512	4,527
Width (mm)	1,923	1,937
Height (mm)	1,214	1,213
Kerb weight (kg)	1,350	1,485

Source: Ferrari press kits

was achieved without the use of any external movable aerodynamic aids.

The new 458 undoubtedly cuts a striking pose, and with a top speed of 202mph (325kph), performance is certainly impressive. Whether this newcomer will win the hearts of the public remains to be seen, but it has the credentials and the gravitas to turn heads – which is just what you would expect from a Ferrari.

↻ Perfect for that weekend get-away in your new 458 Italia, Ferrari offer a set of custom fitted luggage. *(Author)*

↻↻ Located just ahead of the leading edge of the bonnet lid (between the bonnet edge and headlamp) is a narrow air intake which vents air underneath the LED lights and out through the vent on the front wing above the wheel-arch. This air movement is designed to extract the air from the wheel-arch area that causes lift. Feeding air through this narrow slit helps to manage this airflow and reduce lift in the wheel-arch, thereby increasing downforce on Ferrari's new 458 Italia. *(Author)*

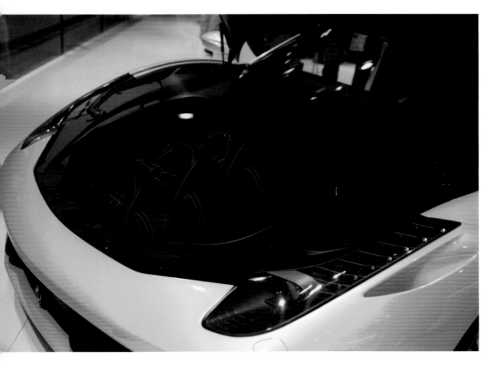

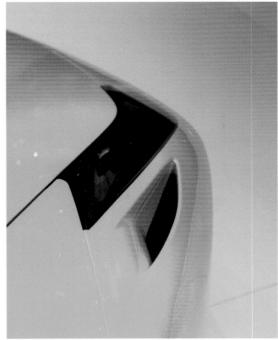

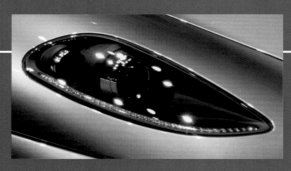

Building on the past

The appeal of Ferrari is very clear in a way, it is about the motor racing heritage and the glamour of the brand. One would say that, at one level, the 'glamour element' is appealing to women.

— NICK MASON
Ferrari owner

Plotting a course for the future

Following the death of Enzo Ferrari in 1988, the company underwent many significant changes, and in the wake of his departure the new President, Luca di Montezemolo, introduced his own style and direction for the future of the company.

In contrast with the modus operandi of the company's founder, di Montezemolo has brought a deep industrial feeling to the brand, increasing the number of models and vehicle production, and this has forced Ferrari to bring its design phase more into line with that of normal road cars in the wider industry.

Today, the company's design research is more of a competition between Ferrari and Pininfarina, with the 'winner' earning the right to proceed with the development. In one sense this has little effect on the outcome of the final design, as collaboration between Ferrari and Pininfarina is very tight anyway.

Car designer Emanuele Nicosia (who worked at Centro Ricerche Pininfarina from 1976 to 1985) said: 'Up until the end of the '80s, Ferrari design and styling never used to follow the general design trends, as any Ferrari model had a unique design which never was "old" or "new" or "advanced"... it was FERRARI!' But Ferraris

today are made for the market rather than being race-inspired as they used to be, the inevitable consequence being that the magic, which those iconic cars of the past had in spades, has been lost. More than one car design professional interviewed for this book agreed that Ferrari designs have now become somewhat predictable, and that market influences and trends could be seen in some of the newer models.

One can divide Ferrari's history into three general periods: the first when Enzo himself ran the show (1940–68); the second when Fiat ruled (1969–91); and the third the current period with Luca di Montezemolo at the helm (1991 to date).

Almost all of the Ferrari cars produced under Enzo's reign have, at the very least, maintained their values, and some models have changed hands at prices that could not have been dreamt of during their production lives. This period was characterised by almost constant economic growth, which provided the funding for consistent success on the track and in the showroom. Although the same design house (Pininfarina) still designs Ferrari's sports cars, it cannot be denied that the most strikingly beautiful and iconic cars came from that era.

During the second period, Fiat controlled much of

○ The F40 is one of Ferrari's most recognisable modern-day classics. *(Author)*

the Ferrari road car development programme, and it is fair to say that by this time Ferrari needed the intervention of a global manufacturer, not least to benefit from the economies of scale that it afforded, and production was increased significantly during this phase. It would, though, be unfair to say that Ferrari produced a range of dull cars under Fiat's parental influence, but apart from such landmark models as the 288 GTO and the F40, this period lacked the real design icons seen in preceding years.

Also, with the exception of the F50 and Enzo models, the years since 1991 have produced few Ferraris with the Wow Factor that came with the introduction of most of Maranello's cars through the 1950s and 1960s. However, without taking anything away from the importance of the reintroduction of Ferrari's front-engined models and di Montezemolo's determination to improve production quality, most of the mid-engined sports cars have followed a theme started by the 308 back in 1975.

The second half of the last century saw most niche or specialist sports car manufacturers having to increase production and/or diversify, because the highly-specialised and limited-production nature of their operations made it more and more difficult to remain in business. What Porsche did in 1983 was to apply the 'Carrera' name, traditionally kept for their highest performing model, to the whole 911 range, with the exception of the Turbo model. In this way they were able to exploit the marketability of that emotional Carrera Panamericana heritage to good effect. While some might argue that it diluted the racing pedigree of the name, it helped the company to survive in difficult times.

Likewise, to increase production, Ferrari capitalised on its vast sporting knowledge and experience by spreading the heritage over a wider product line-up. Shortened design and development phases also helped to keep the brand fresh, even if the model changes were not that significant. The reality was that the romance of thriving on limited production runs was over for Ferrari, and survival had become the name of the game.

As one designer has said, it is the public who decide what is great, not the manufacturer's marketing department, an assertion borne out by the market prices for pre-owned Ferraris. Almost all of the models produced before 1968 have become desirable, yet most of those produced since, with the odd exception mentioned above, have quickly become just used sports cars. However, it is unlikely that Ferrari would have survived to this day without having substantially ramped up production.

Design techniques

Dale Harrow states, 'Twenty years ago people were saying "there is going to be no more hand modelling, there is going to be no more handcraft skills, everything will be on computer." ' It is true that computers have had an enormous effect on the staffing of design studios, but it has not all been doom and gloom. For instance, computer modelling has opened up a whole new world for designers, enabling them to process more work, more quickly. At the same time the need to become skilled in the operation of the complex software has resulted in the development of new training schemes.

While the merits of designing on a screen can be argued, there is no disputing the fact that the use of computers has revolutionised the field of automotive design.

Marián Šuman-Hreblay agrees: 'Electronification and globalisation of corporate automobile design was a great contribution to auto design. Electronic globalisation makes it possible not only to change a basic design for each national market but renders the process relatively easy. Also saved are months of styling and engineering time. This resulted in a decrease in the number of car designers, or those once employed as draftsmen, clay modellers, panelbeaters, etc. Good stylists will always be needed.'

In terms of the design process, one is able to review on screen the changes and modifications to a surface or shape. This can be done in a remarkably short space of time and has led to fewer iterations. It enables a designer to do a quick volume model on screen, perhaps having it milled to get a sense of its proportion before scanning it back into the system, where it can be manipulated to effect further changes. This might then be followed by one or two bigger models, but as Dale Harrow points out: 'There is still the sense that no one is going to sign off a piece of design unless they see it physically, because you cannot really get the same sense of scale, even projecting full size, in animation.'

One of the advantages of using computers in automotive design is that they remove the need to produce physical models at every step of the way, since the modelling process can be left towards the end of the design phase after having explored several options on screen. But Dale Harrow warns: 'You can lose the overall picture very easily looking at it on the screen. Making a quick clay model, you very quickly get used to things like proportion and balance, and overhangs, as those are the building blocks of a successful design. It doesn't matter how well it has been styled if you haven't got the basics right. And I think it is very easy to lose that on a screen.'

In so far as new model research and development projects are concerned, weight reduction has always been a major goal for Ferrari, and on 17 February 2009 the company inaugurated the 'Mille Chili' Laboratory, attached to the Engineering Department at the University of Modena. This consists of a

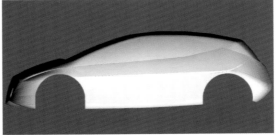

lecture facility equipped with hardware, software, and chassis from Ferrari, with the purpose of enabling eight undergraduates to study research projects aimed at weight reduction. The project's target is for an overall weight of 1,000kg (mille chilli) or below, which serves as a stimulus for the development of lightweight engineering solutions. This ensures an inflow of new ideas for Ferrari, and at the same time contributes to the student's on the job training and experience.

Ferrari marketing

There is something different about a Ferrari. Other high-performance cars may have more power, perhaps a greater top speed, or simply cost more money, but a Ferrari, with the unforgettable high-pitched wail from its 12-cylinder engine, has an elusive mystique and a heritage that evokes passion.

The mystique of Ferrari was quite likely created unintentionally by Enzo Ferrari. He was a guarded and private person, so the industry could not read him in the same way that it could other manufacturers, and the independence of Pininfarina accentuated this. Because he was difficult to predict, everyone was left guessing what his next move would be, and this inevitably attracted more attention to the marque.

Even Ferrari workers would not know what 'Il Commendatore' was thinking until the instruction to build a new model was given to them. With everyone, including the media, left to play the guessing game, Ferrari would repeatedly surprise the world with his new creations, but he could not have done this without a good design house to make his dreams become a reality.

Get a group of motoring enthusiasts together and the conversation will soon turn to matters automotive, and inevitably to Ferrari. But what is it that draws this subject to the surface so often, especially when one considers that Ferrari does no advertising? Nick Mason says, 'In terms of iconic images, I mean "the prancing horse",

Ferrari is up there with Coca Cola. They, of course, don't do billboards and they don't do ads in the papers. Ferrari has always enjoyed a reputation in the market that has almost placed it above advertising, as their exclusivity is what attracted the attention of its customers.'

But that wasn't always the position, as Alfa Romeo, Maserati, and Lamborghini had the measure of Ferrari at various stages over the years. Nick Mason again: 'I think

The Ferrari Magic India Discovery, a 7,000-mile voyage of discovery around the Indian subcontinent in 2008 with two 612 Scagliettis, followed the 60th Anniversary Around-the-World Relay in 2007, the Panamerican 20,000-mile tour in 2006, and the China 15,000 Red Miles tour in 2005. The 612 pictured here is one of the two cars used in the Indian tour, in which the author was given the 'drive of his life' up the Goodwood hill just after the car had returned from India. (Author)

Ferrari just ended up as top dog and the others fell by the wayside, so consequently they have that continuous history of design.'

In an effort to increase awareness of the brand in the emerging markets on the wider international stage, Ferrari have in recent years participated in the much publicised Indian, Panamerican, and Chinese tours, ahead of establishing distribution networks in those countries. Although Ferrari has not stooped to the level of actually advertising its products, it did nevertheless indulge in a spot of brand imaging well before the concept was called brand imaging. Dale Harrow explains: 'Their products were appearing in fantastic movies in the '50s and '60s, and so they did a kind of guerrilla marketing, not a campaign as such, but their cars were everywhere.'

'Ferrari: New Concepts of the Myth'

In January 2005, in an attempt to reinvent itself, Ferrari (in collaboration with Pininfarina) laid down a global challenge, which was called 'Ferrari: New Concepts of the Myth'. They invited universities and design colleges around the world to submit their interpretations of what a future Ferrari should look like. The brief was that the studies should bring innovation in style and function, both externally and internally, and propose stimulating alternatives to the internationally-acclaimed shapes of the current and previous mid-engined 8-cylinder cars and front-engined 12-cylinder cars. Students had total creative freedom, but their designs had to retain the recognisable features and values of the Ferrari marque.

Dale Harrow, Head of Vehicle Design at the Royal College of Art, London, commented, 'They [Ferrari] approached us, but I am always a bit dubious about

competitions like that because it is very hard to understand what companies are looking for. The problem is that they end up getting lots of stuff back and lots of ideas, but so what? What do you do with it all?'

It is evident that, at the time, Ferrari was looking for new ideas outside the organisation, and it is not

⌒ 'Ferrari: New Concepts of the Myth' models on display at the Goodwood Festival of Speed on 8 July 2006 were (in order from the front): Vigore, Avanti, Spirale, Due Masse. *(Author)*

⥀ This model, the Ascari, was one of the four winning models in the 2005 'Ferrari: New Concepts of the Myth' design competition.
(Author)

↻ Another of the four winning models selected by Ferrari in their 'New Concepts of the Myth' design competition. This one is the Fiorano. *(Author)*

↻ In front, the F-Zero model, and behind, the Berlina Sportiva model, both of which were amongst the top 20 finalists in the 'Ferrari: New Concepts of the Myth' design competition, here displayed at the Goodwood Festival of Speed in 2006. *(Author)*

inconceivable that the relationship between Ferrari and Pininfarina had hit 'a wobble as they had been doing the same thing for a long time', as Dale Harrow put it.

The best 20 models in 1:4 scale from four design colleges were put forward for evaluation and were judged by a technical panel including the Ferrari Styling Committee and the senior management of Pininfarina. Four winners were selected and the prize-giving took place in Maranello in November 2005. The winning concepts were the Millechili and Ascari, both from students at the European Institute of Design in Turin, the Fiorano from the Coventry School of Art and Design, and the Tre Diviso from the Tokyo Communication Arts School. The design students responsible for these four models were offered the opportunity of work experience at Ferrari or Pininfarina.

Ferrari's design struggle

In analysing Ferrari's design history, it is difficult not to compare certain iconic models from the past, with which the company enjoyed unbridled supremacy in the sports car market, with those being produced today. It is an unfortunate reality, in today's image-conscious and increasingly pressurised automotive industry, that marketing departments have an ever greater say in what models are produced and what they should look like.

For instance, the Fiat 500 (first produced in July 1957) was one of a number of rear-engined 'small cars' – like the VW Beetle, NSU, and others – that proved to be just the answer in post-war Europe when money and raw materials were in short supply. It was an extremely successful solution to a particular market need at the time, and over the years those cars became icons because the public went for their style and practicality. Today's Fiat 500 is a great little car made to look like the original, but there the similarities end, as even its engine is at the other end of the car, and its sales success today can be put down to a huge marketing campaign more than anything else. Its connection with the original 500 is tenuous at best, and whether it too will become an icon, only time will tell.

In the same way, the Ford Mustang became an overnight success because the market bought into the pony car culture in the early '60s, a cultural phenomenon that faded with time. The idea of recreating modern-day equivalents of these automotive icons, with an expectation of the sales success of the originals, amounts to little more than daydreaming. The market has moved on, and society today has different needs, expectations, and cultural standards. So, is it wise for a company like

◔ **Fiat's legendary 500 – this is the R model from 1972.** *(Archivio e Centro Storico Fiat)*

◒ **The Ford Mustang introduced in 1964 was the fastest-selling motor car ever, selling a million units in its first 18 months of production. The Mustang hit all the right buttons and ticked all the right boxes, giving a hungry younger generation just what they wanted. Ford's research and timing was perfect.** *(Ford Motor Corporation)*

◓ **Set against the backdrop of 16th-century Wilton House, this Ferrari California offers a modern take on classic automotive design.** *(Author)*

Ferrari to try to follow what other manufacturers are doing in the market?

'They probably do it for marketing reasons, but I don't think it is a particularly good route to go and I would rather their new one wasn't called the California, because the California is not an updated version of the original in my opinion, I mean there are too many differences. In the same way, the 288 GTO had very little in common with the original GTO. In particular, the styling is really the thing that you look at when you are tracking a name,' commented Nick Mason.

What made Ferrari successful during the early years in a small and very narrow market niche – one in which its competitors, such as Lamborghini and Maserati, were merely distant also-rans – was that it was consistently good at what it did. Even so, one could ask why, since the other Italian sports car manufacturers had access to the same labour pool and could tap into the same design studios, did Ferrari flourish while the others floundered? The answer is that motor sport played an important role in the testing of components for Ferrari's road cars,

and the numerous successes of Ferraris on the track provided vital PR that in turn helped the company to sell its road cars globally.

Dale Harrow explains: 'They have just been consistently good. It is very hard to look at Ferrari from the 1950s all the way through and find a really bad point in their history. You can't really say they dipped off or have produced a bad car.'

However, like most other cars on the road today, Ferrari have had to accommodate the needs of the modern supercar buyer, who is often someone who can easily afford such a vehicle, but does not necessarily possess the greatest driving skills that this type of car would ordinarily require. The result is that even supercars have had to feature driving aids and creature comforts previously regarded as unthinkable in such a car. Satellite navigation, e-mail, and internet connectivity, as well as the driver's music and entertainment requirements, are now such an important aspect of the modern supercar that these functions are today catered for in complex 'infotainment' centres.

⋂ Although the interior of this **F430 Spider** is businesslike, below the surface is a network of modern electronics which control many of the car's functions. The radio/entertainment centre also doubles up as a satnav display, even if a bit small. *(Author)*

⊃ The famous 'manettino' switch on the steering wheel offers the driver control over the car's dynamic set-up modes according to road conditions: Ice, Low Grip, Sport, and Race. *(Author)*

⌒ At 80 years old, Phil Hill (20 April 1927–28 August 2008) was still driving the Ferraris that he had helped to make famous around the world. Hill did much to bring attention to the Ferrari name in America through his achievements, and at the 2007 Goodwood Revival, a special celebration was held in his honour. He died the following year. *(Author)*

⊃ The 1959 250 GT SWB was one of the models that enabled Ferrari to successfully cross over between road and race car manufacture, as this sports racer could be driven just as easily as an everyday car as it could a fully-fledged racer. The sense of proportion and attitude in this sports car must rank it at the top of the all-time greats. *(Author)*

What does this have to do with car design? Well, it all adds to the car's weight, and over the years additional features such as electric windows, electrically-operated and heated seats, power roof and much more, have collectively resulted in these cars becoming larger. Bigger and heavier cars tend to be slower and, therefore, Ferrari felt the need to produce lighter, stripped-out versions of their road cars, which resulted in the production of the 360 Challenge and others, but this is a reversal of trends for Ferrari. Where, previously, Enzo Ferrari would take a few of his race cars and legalise them for roadgoing purposes, today it is the other way around, where road cars are designed for everyday use, and some of these are singled out for race purposes and put on a severe weight-loss programme to make them competitive.

Perhaps it is this trend that has resulted in the design stagnation of Ferrari's sports cars. 'One of the difficult things in having such a fantastic lineage of brilliant cars, is where do you find the space in that situation to look beyond to what Ferrari could be in the future? I can quite understand, if you have got a very good process that works and produces great cars, how difficult it might be to force change from within,' observed Dale Harrow.

The 2005 'Ferrari: New Concepts of the Myth' competition referred to above might well have been an attempt by Ferrari to gain some new ideas in their quest for that elusive creative theme that would take them forward. For, whilst during the '50s and '60s each new model drew gasps of admiration and envy from Ferraristi, motoring enthusiasts, and even the motor

industry, the design and styling of their sports cars had latterly become somewhat predictable. Perhaps this was because the company had deviated from its original raison d'être, which was to produce race cars from which a limited number of road cars would follow.

Although this formula would not work today, the fact remains that Ferrari's core focus appears somewhat greyed when looking at the company's recent design direction, with successive models seeming to be little more than variations on a theme. Surely, at the pinnacle of the industry, there is plenty of scope to push the envelope with fresh designs.

During the '50s, '60s, and even the '70s, Ferrari was anything but predictable – the company was innovative and almost daring. Dale Harrow says, 'I would agree with that. There was a whole series of cars [at a later stage] that were not only predictable, but aesthetically they were actually not very nice, and you can see that there was something wrong there with their relationship [with Pininfarina].'

'The public take products for what they are, and I think it is probably fair to say that a lot of companies do have their golden age. And I think that if one looks at Ferrari and you look back at the golden age of Ferrari and their designs, then it does go through phases, and in some cases [their cars] are just more sexy and more desirable, and more emotive than others. And that has to do with the designers. But, ultimately, if the punters decide that, then now is probably not a golden period for Ferrari because that lusting for the brand that once existed is no longer evident. People now are bowing to the Prancing Horse, and the image, and the name, rather than the vehicle,' observed Keith Helfet.

Scratching beneath the surface of both Ferrari and Pininfarina, one would surely find them no different from any other big manufacturing organisation, and it is reasonable to assume that they would have suffered from the same type of corporate politics as any other large corporation.

With Ferrari at the top of their client list, design jobs at Pininfarina were highly sought after. Indeed, doors worldwide would be open to any designer able to say on their curriculum vitae that they had worked on Ferraris at Pininfarina. So in-house competition for Ferrari design projects was very tough, and it was inevitable that internal politics would create some turmoil amongst the staff, which in turn seemed to result in signs of design stagnation. It is this that was thought to have led to the

'Ferrari: New Concepts of the Myth' competition in 2005. But, as Dale Harrow points out, 'If something is seen to have been influenced by a student project, what does that say about an international company like Ferrari?'

During the time that Ferrari was experiencing this lack of design direction, the likes of Aston Martin and Bentley were redefining themselves, and taking a long

⊃ **Ferrari's 250 GTL Lusso combined great sportiness with elegance. The design of the GTL was highly acclaimed as it offered excellent visibility through the extensive glass area, making it a practical all-round performer.** *(Author)*

hard look internally at what the company and the brand actually meant, but, according to Harrow, there was no evidence of that going on at Ferrari.

'It would have been interesting to see if in-house they were thinking "well, is Ferrari just a red car", or "what are we about", because I think they were a bit lost, actually. Also, I don't really think they are producing beautiful cars anymore. I think Aston Martin has done it, in a way, and that will be, I imagine, why most people buy those cars – because they are beautiful. They only consider afterwards if they are Aston Martins, as they are drawn by the beauty of the car, and I don't think they [Ferrari] have got that at the moment. I mean, the latest California is just terrible,' Dale Harrow said.

➲ Ferrari's California received a mixed response from professional designers and press alike, but it still offers a commanding presence. *(Author)*

Keith Helfet agrees, 'I think the general consensus is that the current Ferraris are not considered with the same awe as they were in previous times, and I think that says something about the current design. Whoever is designing them needs to take responsibility for that. You know, we [as professional designers] are judged by our output, and I think the punters have spoken fairly clearly because I don't see any evidence of that awe that used to be around Ferrari design. You know, the 308 and 328 days – that really was a magnificent period. I don't think the current cars are a patch on those cars. And I think most of the classic Ferraris are the ones that are much more sculptured than the present lot. They used form, and were sexier. The 308 had certain two-dimensional panels, but the rest was just gorgeous with its proportions, same as the 328. I think that most companies now have virtually unlimited design resources, so if their design is not up to scratch, they have got no excuses.'

The way racing influences design has been touched on, and the argument has been put forward that Ferrari's motor sport programme of the '50s and '60s provided design crossover for its road-going cars. In response to this, Keith Helfet says, 'Probably, but that crossover was fairly loose because in a way these things are all done for the right reasons. When I designed the Jaguar XJ220, we started off designing it as a Group B race car, and it was a very interesting exercise, because I was working with racing people and doing things differently.'

Ferrari have always prided themselves on being a forward-looking company. Enzo Ferrari was not even the slightest bit interested in last year's model – he always looked towards the next car. That was all very well while they were producing some of the world's finest sports cars, but with the current trend of many similar and not the best-looking models the company has put its name to, perhaps it would make sense to draw some inspiration from a few of their greatest early examples.

Dale Harrow says, 'I think it is a bit of a shame they are not bringing that heritage and tradition into their new products, and have resisted actually dipping into their history. You could imagine them going back to some of those '50s and '60s models and reinterpreting them just like Aston Martin have done. They have gone back and kind of found that [design] language and kind of tweaked it.'

The success of many of the older Ferraris perhaps highlights the fact that a lot of the design back then was successful because it was done in an atmosphere of relative freedom. Dale Harrow goes on to say, 'Yes, I think that is true as well. And I think the current designs have got lost in a poor aesthetic collection of shapes that they just keep reinterpreting, when actually there is more in the cupboard. And I am surprised that Ferrari has not gone back and looked in that cupboard, because you could almost imagine they could hatch a stream of heritage vehicles, limited editions, and make some very serious money and actually redefine themselves a little bit by actually doing that.'

Research has shown that people's taste is usually set early on in their lives, and that they tend to keep their early preferences thereafter. This makes it all the more surprising that Ferrari have not analysed their heritage more actively, since many of those motoring enthusiasts who, when they were young, dreamed about one day owning their favourite Ferrari sports car are now (if they have been successful in business) in a position to afford one. Keith Helfet shares his feelings: 'I resent what's happening at the moment because when I couldn't afford the cars that I desired, there were a lot of them around to choose from. Now that I can afford one, there is nothing that I really want. There are still key cars that I yearn for, and the 328 is one of them. If I were looking for a Ferrari, that's the car I'd still buy now, and in a way that says it all.'

However, the dynamics of the market have changed substantially from the days when designers produced sports cars that had real meaning for both the company and the car's owner. That is to say that the owner of a Ferrari in the period between the '50s and perhaps the '80s was more likely to have been a motor sport enthusiast who would have been swayed by Ferrari's racing results around the world.

With the increase in the number of models now available, and therefore in total production, a greater

➲ **The Ferrari F430 is today perhaps one of the most complete sports cars, offering quality, reliability, and performance. This Spider was shown at the 2008 Geneva Motor Show.**
(Author)

⌒ **Ferrari's 612 Scaglietti has been around since 2004, but a replacement is expected in 2011.** *(Author)*

number of Ferrari sports cars will today be purchased by customers who show little or no interest in the company's heritage, and have no intention of driving their car competitively. It is therefore fair to say that the purpose of the sports car at this level has changed to one that appeals to the affluent seeking a status symbol, rather than the enthusiast looking to compete on the track.

Emanuele Nicosia sees it this way: 'Because of the increasingly sophisticated and crowded supercar market, Ferrari needs to be a special creature. The battle, or fight, with other supercars to stay ahead of the game could one day go Ferrari's way, and the other day it could swing the way of the competition, but this would merely bring Ferrari down to the same level as all the other cars.'

Ferrari has a heritage of more than half a century of building the finest sports cars in the world, and it has unrivalled Formula 1 experience and all the technical knowledge that comes from successfully competing in countless different race categories around the world.

A passionate Emanuele Nicosia outlines the road ahead: 'A Ferrari needs to communicate its soul, it needs to have a relationship with its driver, like with its designer … it is a question of an emotional relationship that starts with the designer, engineers, and mechanics, and continues until it reaches the final owner, who has to be in love with his Ferrari. He has to love his Ferrari because of the emotion of driving, the continuous communication with his car, bend after bend, straight after straight. Like a person, like a friend, they will know each other better and better with time, always increasing the pleasure of the emotional feeling. This is what a designer has to feel when he starts to use his hands, his brain, and his soul at the start of the design phase and afterwards, throughout the development of the car.'

Still very active in the world of Italian design, Nicosia feels that Ferrari should have fewer models, perhaps two GT Berlinettas and two roadster versions. The two GTBs should follow the true racing concept closely connected with Formula 1 cars and GT championship racing, and this means one mid-engined and one front-engined. The softer and more elegant models would be the roadster versions.

Styling need be neither classical nor radical, but it should epitomise the car's true racing soul rather than follow market trends. Meanwhile, for some special models, Ferrari could once again adopt a sub-brand, like it did with the Dino 206/246, without affecting the main Ferrari brand strategy.

Conclusion

During his time, Enzo Ferrari was a unique figure in the auto industry. 'Il Commendatore' was his own man in every respect, a one-off original just like many of his early cars, and he constantly moved forward because his next model was always going to be his best model.

'In the end, design must come down to personality; that is what design is all about, it is someone's expression. And if that turns out to be a committee, the design usually ends up as a bit more of a compromise, so ultimately it is management and those people involved who have to be responsible and accountable,' Keith Helfet concludes.

It has been said that Ferrari have always had a style of their own, a style that has portrayed a pleasing balance between elegance and simplicity. But this factor in the

equation was down to the quality of Pininfarina's design as much as it was Enzo's insistence that his cars would always be the best. It must be said that for a Ferrari to be a Ferrari sports car, it should always possess a certain degree of arrogance. Their cars should never be led by marketing trends, for that would make them like the rest of the industry, and the cars from Maranello would lose their unique character. That would be to lose Ferrari altogether.

⋂ **Lady in the window – about to pilot a super-rare 250 GTO around Goodwood. She manages a quick smile before the off.** *(Author)*

Bibliography

Batchelor, Dean and Leffingwell, Randy, *Ferrari Buyer's Guide* (Motorbooks International USA, 1996).

Beehl, Nathan, *Ferrari Supercars* (Guild Publishing London, 1986).

Burgess-Wise, David, *Ghia, Ford's Carrozzeria – A study of one of Italy's oldest and finest coachbuilders* (Osprey Publishing, 1985).

Grayson, Stan, *Ferrari – The Man, the Machines, Automobile Quarterly* (Princeton Publishing, 1975).

Haajanen, Lennart W., *Illustrated Dictionary of Automobile Body Styles* (McFarland & Company Inc., 2003).

Lewin, Tony and Borroff, Ryan, *How to Design Cars Like a Pro – A Comprehensive Guide to Car Design from the Top Professionals* (Motorbooks International USA, 2003).

Ludvigsen, Karl, *Ferrari – 60 Years of Technological Innovation* (Ferrari S.p.A, 2007).

Mondadori, Arnoldo and Nada, Giorgio, *Ferrari – All the Cars* (Haynes Publishing, 2005).

Pininfarina: Art and Industry 1930–2000 (Pininfarina S.p.A., 2000).

Sparke, Penny, *A Century of Car Design* (Mitchell Beazley, 2002).

Šuman-Hreblay, Marián, *Dictionary of World Coachbuilders and Car Stylists*.

Tipler, Johnny, *La Carrera Panamericana, The World's Greatest Road Race* (Veloce Publishing, 2008).

Tumminelli, Paolo, *Car Design* (teNeues Publishing Group, 2004).

Magazines

Autocar – various.

CAR (United Kingdom) – various.

CAR (South Africa) – various.

Road & Track – various.

Supercar Classics – various.

Index

Page numbers in *italics* refer to illustration captions.